still waters

A PORTRAIT OF BROADLAND TODAY

By MILES HEDLEY

Photographs by
DAVID KOPPEL

MAAS BOOKS

Published in Great Britain in 1999
by
Maas Books
62 Manor Road
Barnet, Herts EN5 2LF

ISBN 0 9535492 0 8

Printed and bound in Great Britain
by
Page Bros, Mile Cross Lane,
Norwich NR6 6SA

For Charmaine

one

I went out to buy a waterproof jacket and came back with a 16ft canoe. I couldn't help it. I saw it in a shop, a sleek, green, shiny marvel, and I just had to have it. But how was I to explain to my long-suffering family that I could not live without a canoe, even though our home was in the suburbs of London and my working life was spent in a concrete office block in the East End?

On the return journey, the boat strapped to the roof of my car, I had an inspiration: I would say I was going to write a book about a canoe trip through Broadland - after all, I had been visiting the Broads for more than 30 years and had always said how much I would like to see my name on a dust-cover. This outburst provoked a rash of raised eyebrows and left me with only two choices: to admit the canoe was a shopaholic aberration or to take their scepticism as a challenge. Thank God, I chose the latter.

Over the next two years, I spent almost all my spare time abroad on the broads in my canoe. At first, it was enough simply to paddle aimlessly along the waterways, learning to read tide tables to avoid fighting against the current, exploring wondrously peaceful backwaters too shallow for bigger boats and discovering how to circumvent the stretches of water that became chockablock at the height of the holiday season. But quite soon, I realised that the real joy of Broadland lay not just in its scenic beauty but in its inhabitants. Chance meetings showed me that the area was awash with fascinating characters, all of them with stories to tell. And the more people I met, the more I came to understand how perilously fragile an environment the Broads of Norfolk and Suffolk have become.

Mankind has roamed these flat but exquisite wetlands for 250 millennia. For all but the last tiny handful of years, our forebears have worked hand in glove with nature, helping her create the landscape of river, lake, marsh and meadow spread out beneath enormous skies and ringed with hazy horizons whose lines are broken only by the silhouettes of church, mill and tree (let's forget pylons for the time being). The 20th century, however, with its stupefying advances in science and commerce, has wrought more damage on the ecology than any ice age or sea-flood; and it has brought the broads to the threshhold of catastrophe.

Barney Matthews

The reasons are legion. Nearly three-quarters of Broadland is agricultural, and developments in fertilisers to increase productivity have led to alarming quantities of nitrogen-rich effluents leaching into the waterways. The rivers and broads are also bombarded with phosphates that pour in from domestic waste. The result is eutrophication, a superabundance of nutrients creating a population explosion of algae, whose colonies cloud the water so comprehensively that plant-life is suffocated, fish are killed, insects are obliterated and birds are driven to new feeding grounds.

The problem does not even end there. Water boards abstract the life-blood of Broadland, reducing river flows and thus opening the floodgates to increasing salination as salt tides surge in from the North Sea. And the demands of tourism - the financial life-blood of the region - mean more and bigger boats, with the attendant damage caused by fuel spills and by bank erosion from their washes.

Tourism brings a million visitors a year to the Broads. Boating alone accounts for nearly 6,000 jobs, directly or indirectly, and pumps more than £15million into the local economy. But it also brings the danger of saturation. There are some 14,000 boats registered on the Broads, an average of more than a hundred vessels for every mile of navigable water. Tolls produce about £1million annually and pay for some of the aquatic maintenance that such numbers necessitate. But it is only a fraction of the sum required.

Lottery money and grants from Westminster and the European Union are easing the burden; the latter, for example, has given £1.5million for reedbed restoration in an attempt to lure back to

Broadland the elusive bittern, a rare heron-like bird that has become a symbol of the battle to save the wetland. An array of "green" designations, each bringing domestic or European funding, has also helped. But the classifications are bewildering - ESA, SSSI, Ramsar, SPA, SAC, NNR - and some lack sufficient statutory clout.

The administration of Broadland is equally confounding. The region has national park status; but this is no eco-Eden, for its charter insists that its overlords "protect" the interests of navigation, which are not always the same as those of conservation. The region is run under the auspices of the Broads Authority, whose ranks, quite properly and democratically, include almost every vested interest in the area. But rule by committee is axiomatically fraught; for example, plans for the use of water - Broadland's most vital commodity - may be subject to the agreement of more than ten separate parties.

Ecology versus economy, long-termism versus short-termism - these are the dilemmas that face those entrusted with the future of the Broads.

In the end, long-term ecological arguments simply have to prevail if the wetland is to survive. More than 250 species of plant yet remain. There are also tens of thousands of birds - many of them distressingly rare - dozens of species of mammal, countless insects and a plethora of fish that make the Broads the top coarse-fishing destination in Britain. But pollution, eutrophication, boat numbers, sewage, water abstraction and industrial effluent (including, incredibly, mercury that was dumped legally in the Yare) are colossal threats whose defeat will cost millions of pounds, money that is not as yet forthcoming.

Money is needed, too, for the non-aquatic attractions of Broadland. There are scores of ancient mills and hundreds of other historic buildings - 140 of Britain's 179 round-tower churches are in Norfolk - and many are in need of repair. There are also some 200 miles of rights of way that require constant care, as well as vast tracts of overgrown fen and carr (woodland floating on a crust of peat above reservoirs of liquid mud) and pollution-threatened oceans of reed that once provided a livelihood for generations of locals.

The broads - forty-odd remain - were created when a rise in sea-levels in the 14th century led to the flooding of medieval peat-diggings in the valleys of the region's six rivers: the Bure, Ant, Thurne, Yare, Chet and Waveney. Today, there is a real danger of a second, lethal inundation; not one caused by a new rise in sea-levels (although global warming makes this is a serious risk) but by the headlong tide of progress.

The basic question, I suppose, is this: are the broads worth preserving? Some say man is fighting a losing battle against the sea that no amount of concrete shore-defences can ultimately halt. This camp might take as its motto Noel Coward's sublimely dismissive, "Very flat, Norfolk". But surely the answer has to be yes, for this precious biological gem is, in the words of the great Broadland naturalist and poet Ted Ellis, "a breathing space for the cure of souls."

This book is in part the story of a canoe journey through the waterways of this impoldered region, in part an unashamed hymn to its beauty and to the people who live and work amid its wonders. It records the fears and dreams of some of the men and women whom I was fortunate enough to encounter on my travels and it chronicles their struggle to preserve their birthright from destruction. Sometimes their stories are sad; but almost without exception, these Broadland devotees retain a dauntlessly optimistic passion for the region that forces me to believe, as I write on the eve of a new millennium, that salvation is not yet out of reach. The Broads, as a thatcher remarked to me, may not yet have turned the corner; but they have turned a corner.

two

Coltishall is as pleasant a riverside town as it is possible to find. The streets are lined with attractive Georgian buildings, many built of red brick with delicately latticed bow windows. The church of St John the Baptist is, like many of its county counterparts, thatched with reed. It also contains an architectural rarity: two Saxon windows in the north wall. But because Coltishall owes its existence to the Bure, it is on the riverbank that its true heart lies. The grassy, tree-spangled staithe, overlooked by a magnificent white-stuccoed Palladian house and an attractive olde worlde pub, offers many mooring spots among the ducks, geese and swans that throng the water waiting for scraps from holidaymakers.

This is a splendid spot to begin a tour of the Broads, for Coltishall, in its heyday, was the birthplace of one of the most culturally important facets of Broadland life, the wherry, the great fore-and-aft-rigged freighter that, with the similarly rare bittern, is such a potent symbol of these shallow, tidal and often brackish waterways.

Wherries, with their vast black sails, first appeared in the 17th century and, like so much in the Broads, owed their innovative design, allowing them to sail close to the wind, to the Dutch, who had already taught Norfolk the subtle art of digging the drainage dykes that enabled land lying below sea level to be reclaimed for agriculture and gave the area its most distinctive feature: levees embanking the rivers several feet above the surrounding ground, which creates the delightful trompe l'oeil effect of boats sailing across fields.

Some of these wherries, particularly those that regularly went to sea, were true leviathans: Wonder, the biggest of them all, weighed 80 tons. Others, designed specifically for the winding, shoal-ridden waters of small rivers such as the Ant, were little more than one-man barges: Cabbage, for instance, could carry only four tons of cargo. Coltishall's most famous yard was Allens, which flourished in the second half of the 19th century, making one wherry a year. That may not sound much but the skill in building these clinker-built marvels of oak, often with mahogany trimmings, is immense. Allens' boats, with their gaily-painted masts, were considered the sleekest produced in Norfolk, a reputation put to the test in regular races and in the day-to-day cut-throat competition of rival builders, of whom Halls of Reedham were the main threat, for their wherries were reputedly the fastest ever made.

River trading, which was carried on by some 300 wherries at their peak in the Victorian era, had been unchallenged for centuries; but it was wiped out almost at a stroke by the arrival of the railways in the 1880s. Until then, roads were almost non-existent and rivers, dominated by wherry skippers, were the life-blood of the villages that clustered on their banks. Wherrymen supplied, through the ports of Great Yarmouth and, later, Lowestoft, such essentials as coal, fish, oil, salt, pitch, bricks and timber. Trains carried the same cargoes - but in far greater bulk and at far greater speed. The first track, a 15-inch narrow-gauge line, was laid between 1878 and 1880 to link Coltishall with Aylsham and Wroxham, which in turn had connections to Norwich and thence to Britain's industrial heartland and to London. As early as 1900, the number of trading wherries had fallen by two-thirds. The last to be built, Ella, was launched in 1912 by Allens.

The 19th century may have ended disastrously for wherry-builders but, initially at least, it turned Coltishall into a boom town. At its zenith, Coltishall boasted nine pubs, a cattle market, several limeworks fed by the region's many chalk quarries, numerous maltings, a railway station and, of course, its boatyards. But the passing of the wherry also heralded a decline in its other trades. One by one, the kilns were extinguished and by 1927 the last maltings had vanished. As a commercial concern, the railway struggled on; but it closed to passengers in 1952 and to freight thirty years later. It was reopened in 1990 as a tourist route and does a roaring trade again.

The revolutionary effect of industrial advancement on the peaceful, bucolic backwaters of Norfolk was matched only by the attrition of natural forces. Elemental strife is something Broadlanders have learned to accept in their windswept flatlands; devastating floods have wreaked regular havoc since Man first set foot here. A particularly savage inundation in 1912 - the year of the last trading wherry - swept away the old bridge that had spanned the Bure at Coltishall for centuries and wrecked 12 miles of navigation to Aylsham. The bridge was replaced within a year; navigation for anything except dinghies was never restored and Aylsham was cut off from the wherry traders.

Today, Coltishall's main concerns are tourism and the Royal Air Force. The RAF has a base on the edge of town, home to some fifty Jaguar warplanes and up to 800 service personnel and their families. It was also home for a time to the legendary Battle of Britain fighter pilot Group Captain Douglas Bader.

For those in anything bigger than a dinghy, the only way to go from Coltishall is downstream. Travellers in small boats, however, can head upstream, beyond the boundaries of the national park, where the river is a veritable potamic Elysium. Aylsham has an effulgent literary heritage: It was the home, and property, of John of Gaunt - son of Edward III and patron of Chaucer - who was immortalised by Shakespeare and given the most beautiful and ironic speech in the language, the one that features:

This royal throne of kings, this sceptr'd isle,
This earth of majesty, this seat of Mars,
This other Eden, demi-paradise,
This fortress built by Nature for herself
Against infection and the hand of war,
This happy breed of men, this little world,
This precious stone set in a silver sea...

Downsteam from Coltishall, the Bure is limpid and peaceful. Leaving the staithe, the banks soon become fringed with willow, alder and sallow, making it lousy for sailing but perfect for those of us who rely on muscle. The water is almost transparent and thick with weeds, among which dart shoals of roach and minnow. Coot, moorhen, mallard, mute swan and great crested grebe breast the wind-ruffled shallows; in the spring, these latter stage one of the most wondrous of all avian mating rituals, a graceful water-borne pas-de-deux of pirouettes, shimmies and harmonic twists and dips that only a Pavlova or Fonteyn could hope to emulate and that would leave Esther Williams looking as ungainly as a duck out of water.

A fabulous treat now awaits: the impossibly picturesque crenellated tower of St Peter's church at Belaugh rises above the trees, its reflection in the water reducing its stolid squareness into insubstantial wafts. The church has its own tiny staithe with a pilgrims' path connecting the two. But the better approach is from Belaugh's public staithe, equally small, which stands at the bottom of a surprisingly steep lane, more like Devon than Norfolk, flanked by ancient cottages that create a lovely frame for the house of worship that looms above them. St Peter's has a Norman nave and chancel and a fine 15th century painted screen that was defaced in 1643 by a "godly trooper", one of Cromwell's iconoclastic fundamentalist thugs who laid waste in the cause of monotonous Puritanism so much of our polychrome past.

Back on the river, the trees on the right conceal a Broadland eccentricity. Chalk for the limekilns of Coltishall was dug out for hundreds of years, the last quarry finally going out of business in 1877. These pits have, in the years since, become overgrown with carr and undergrowth, leaving a landscape of verdant tumps and hollows that locals, with nice hyperbole, nicknamed Little Switzerland. The epithet stuck and now graces the Ordnance Survey map.

The Bure at this point meanders in such a loop that it almost touches Belaugh again, passing on the left the private and gated Belaugh Broad, dredged and cleared by the Broads Authority in 1987 and invisible among the trees. As I paddled along this reach on a clear autumn afternoon, an osprey suddenly appeared from above the trees and swooped low over the water, passing so close to my canoe that I could almost have touched it.

The river straightens out as it runs towards Wroxham, the first glimpse of which comes with St Mary's church atop a grassy acclivity on the starboard side. The architectural historian Nikolaus Pevsner, who carried out a unique, not to say Herculean, labour by visiting and describing almost every building of note in England, was delighted by the "barbaric and glorious" Norman porch.

Bridge Broad, a tranquil oasis taking its name from the railway bridge that spans the Bure here, also lies to the right and marks the end of one of the most peaceful - and most easily canoed - stretches of water in the whole region. A stone's throw further on is Wroxham old bridge, a narrow stone arch built in 1614, widened in 1894 and survivor of everything nature could throw at it.

Properly, the left bank is a separate town, Hoveton, which has its own parish church, 13th century St John's, and a little thatched chapel called St Peter's, with pews for some four dozen worshippers in a whitewashed interior lit by unstained glass windows. But Wroxham and Hoveton are, in reality, one settlement today, with the bridge surrounded by new developments of hotels, holiday homes, boat-hire offices, restaurants and shops - most of which are called Roys.

Roys describes itself as the biggest village shop in the world. The main street boasts Roys department store, Roys supermarket, Roys boutique, Roys garden shop, Roys DIY store... the list goes on. The business was actually founded in Coltishall in 1895 and run by the brothers Arnold and Alfred Roy and their sister. Arnold, who once hawked oranges around Norfolk with a donkey called William, was bursting with Victorian entrepreneurial zeal and quickly realised that tourism in the Broads was the future. He moved the business to Wroxham in 1904, offered boating parties provisions that he would take back if they were unused and by the 1930s was attracting 200,000 customers a year. That single tiny store has grown into a miniature empire.

Arnold's faith in a touristic future was based on the coming of the railway and the success of a Norwich man called John Loynes. Loynes had moved to Wroxham from the county town where, in 1878, he had started a hire business with a 14ft wooden rowing boat that he had restored himself. His Wroxham boatyard was a huge success and enabled him to expand into Europe, although his operation in the Netherlands crashed at the turn of the century as a result of Dutch fury at Britain's treatment of the Boers. The tourism boom led to an explosion of new boatyards. Many still exist today but usually in name only because so many have been taken over by large-scale holiday operators. Loynes' own yard, for example, is now owned by Broads Tours, which is part of the Funnell Group run by Len and Hazel Funnell, their son Mark and daughter Ruth.

Hazel, who has been in the fleet business for more than two decades, is weary of hearing some people accuse boat-owners and farmers of harming the Broads in pursuit of ever-greater profits. The problems, she is quick to emphasise, are more complex than that and "blaming" will not help address them. "The Broads have national park status, which means that conservation, navigation" - heavily stressed - "and quiet enjoyment should have equal priority. But they don't seem to in reality."

Hazel Funnell

The navigation budget for vital river work such as dredging and clearing comes from annual boat tolls which, in 1997, generated about £1million. Tolls for hire companies are three times higher than for private owners. "If we weren't here," Hazel said, "employment would be severely hit, the boatbuilding trade would be greatly diminished and the Broads would be in danger of silting up. There would also be many other problems if too many boats were kept off the water."

Tourism - a term essentially synonymous with the fleet industry - provides almost 6,000 jobs locally and pumps more than £15million into the local economy. "The Broads were created for economic reasons as peat-diggings, so economic activities are not new," said Hazel. She is a member of BEEN, the Broads Environmental Education Network, and regularly takes local children on day-trips. She told me: "When I first went to a BEEN meeting, I felt like a murderer going among sheep. But I was surprised by the warmth of the welcome I received. The general thought seems to be that because you run a business you are not interested in the environment. But the reverse is true because our greatest asset is the broads themselves. Clean, pristine and healthy water is as vital for us as for everyone else because without it, holidaymakers would not come here to enjoy the Broads."

She and her husband started out with fewer than a dozen boats but now have about a hundred; and Broads Tours is the second biggest fleet firm in the area after Richardsons of Stalham. Many small businesses have been swallowed up in the previous decade. Hazel said: "Boat-hire businesses have been decimated in the past ten years; their numbers are down probably threefold. Taxes, rates and insurance keep going up but holiday income has stayed the same."

The secret to successful management of the Broads, Hazel believes, lies in communication. She said: "It would be nice if equal notice was taken of locals - especially 'old' locals who have experienced the changes on the Broads - and academics. It would be nice, too, to have more discussions between academics who hold different opinions. But things are changing. People are working together and organisations like BEEN are vital. I'm optimistic. Prejudices are being averted by face-to-face meetings, not confrontations."

But Hazel is in no doubt that the road ahead is a hard one. She said: "We have tried introducing an electric cruiser into our fleet but we could not let it out. People are nervous of new technology and want freedom but they feel restricted because they know they have to get to a charging point each day. We converted it to diesel mid-season and it was fully booked for the rest of the year.

"We are considering cruisers that combine electric and diesel power and we are bringing back sail as well. It's historical, although even sailing boats at speed make a lot of wash which worsens bank erosion. But there is some gorgeous sailing in this area and, after all, variety is the joy of the Broads."

Hazel's quest for that most delicate of balances between economy and ecology has not always been appreciated. She said: "When we built our offices in Wroxham we pulled down some horrible old corrugated iron sheds that flooded in winter while our men were working there. But some people criticised us for destroying the character of the Broads. We must be forward-looking. I hope that planning controls will not make the area too chocolate-boxy. We should be encouraging architects to use traditional materials for new Norfolk designs. We should have faith in our architects - there is never only one view of what is tasteful."

Innovation is essential for progress - but no one can dispute that there will always remain a place for tradition. And this great virtue is personified by Peter Bower and Barney Matthews at the Wherry Yacht Charter boatyard just a short paddle from the Broads Tours' headquarters. When I first met Peter he looked, in PG Wodehouse's wonderful phrase, like an owl with a secret sorrow. Changing holiday patterns, already discussed by Hazel, had meant that bookings were down and their profit for that month was a princely £8.33p; bad enough for most but potentially catastrophic for a firm that owns a wherry and two wherry yachts, a trio of almost century-old miracles of the boatbuilder's art that require a terrifying amount of maintenance. Peter's melancholy is ingenuous - but it vanishes the moment Barney appears. One moment he was talking in atrabilious tones about the return of the yobbos to the Broads thanks to cheap offers in newspapers, the next he was wiping away tears of laughter as Barney regaled him with some tale of ferocious obscenity. It was like sunshine after the storm as Barney, a former mining engineer and old Africa hand with a penchant for Brahms and Churchill, turned an outpouring of depression into the greatest

comedy double act since Eric and Ernie. As we photographed them at their yard, Barney, adopting a glorious mock-Victorian pose, dissolved into giggles as Peter broke into a rendering of Mr Wonderful; moments later, Peter was reduced to uncontrollable hysteria as Barney, turning his filthy flat cap back to front like some streetwise teenager, peered into the camera's viewfinder and took his partner's photograph. The constant ribbing, of course, reveals a deep affection. Barney said: "We really get on very well together. We sometimes have a swearing match but it is nothing personal." But their friendship was crystallised for me when Barney, in a moment of unusual seriousness, said: "I've given the last 12 years of my life to this." "Don't say last," Peter interrupted quietly, "say past."

This odd couple linked their fortunes in 1984, having previously been fighting single-handed battles to preserve their boats. Barney, never to be seen without a pipe or roll-up cigarette in his mouth, bought his 1912 wherry yacht, Norada, in 1964 on the proceeds of his African adventures. "She cost me £1,800," he said, "which was about the same as a bungalow at the time." Peter, a former school teacher, bought his own wherry yacht, Olive, in 1974 "because I had to". These two boats, custom-built for the Edwardian tourist boom in the Broads, were crafted from oak, mahogany, brass and leather and need constant TLC. Barney had already spent £40,000 on Norada when he teamed up with Peter; Peter devoted his out-of-school hours to Olive, restoring her to her original 1909 specifications. He said: "It soon became obvious that I would have to charter her to keep her going." His first season in business, 1978, proved that he was on to something. He said: "I carried on teaching full-time until 1986 and spent all my spare time on Olive. Meanwhile I had met up with Barney. We just hit it off and formed the Wherry Yacht Charter in 1984. The following winter Hathor came up for sale. We had to have her."

Even a cursory glance shows why. Hathor, a 24-ton wherry named after the Egyptian goddess of love, was built as a pleasure boat by Halls of Reedham in 1905 for the sisters Ethel and Helen Colman, daughters of the great Norwich mustard dynasty. They commissioned her in memory of their brother, who died of tuberculosis while cruising on the Nile in a boat also called Hathor. The magnificent teak interior is panelled with sycamore inlaid with Egyptian motifs of Hathor herself, crocodiles, lotus flowers and scarabs, many deep-stained red and green. "The trouble is," Peter said, "sycamore is a lousy wood for boats because it is prone to damp, rot and woodworm and needs a hell of a lot of looking after. But it was designed by an architect, not a boatbuilder. When we got her, she needed a two-year restoration."

The restoration was uncompromising and Hathor emerged fitted out almost exactly as she was when she first slipped into the River Yare. That means no mod cons such as showers - a decision that is now beginning to take a toll. Peter said: "People have to make do and wait till we tie up somewhere that has a shower block. At first, it didn't matter but in the past ten years all that has changed. There is too much mollycoddling today."

Too much mollycoddling - and too much loutism. Peter's expression becomes splenetic again. "The kiss-me-quick brigade are told to come and have a booze-up for next to nothing. I thought those days were gone for ever and I can't bear the thought of the yobbos coming back. Twenty years ago it was very bad but until recently it had got so much better. I'm not obsessed with money" - understatement of the year - "but if I can't enjoy what I do any more then there is no point going on." He smiled sadly. "I'm feeling very cynical at the moment; perhaps it will be better in a couple of weeks."

In fact, the mood lifted within a couple of minutes as Barney reduced him to helpless laughter with another of his outrageous stories. Trying to keep a straight face, Peter said: "I'm optimistic about lots of things. The water quality is much better than it was, kids on the whole are great and the people who have been coming to the Broads in recent years are terrific. They lowered the speed limits a few years ago and that made a lot of difference. I thought 'This is great.' But after a while they started creeping up again."

The speed limits rarely exceed 4mph and are generally 3mph on built-up reaches of the rivers and on the broads. They are policed by river inspectors aboard launches. But Peter believes more should be done. "The inspectors should also be hiding on the banks with radar guns. And it's pointless fining tourists - the boatyards should pay. But there are too many vested interests and too many influential people are irresponsible, charging down the river at full throttle."

Peter Bower and Barney Matthews

When I visited the Wherry Yacht Charter some months later, Peter's Jeremiad proved to have been justified - 1997 was not a good year. It was not helped when a cross-wind snapped Hathor's huge tree-trunk mast. Modern glues enabled it to be repaired and Peter reflected with a wry smile: "I must be the only living wherryman to have broken one of these monsters." But things were looking up for the following season, with several bookings already in place.

Peter, who worked on the railways before becoming a teacher, also has a miniature railway laid out next to his boatyard. It is open to the public in the season - but it makes no contribution to the wherry business's coffers because every penny it raises is given to charity. Peter said: "We are still in financial trouble and we need outside help. There are only the two of us and we are too busy to go out fund-raising, setting up trusts and so on, although we may have to. But I won't put sponsorship logos on the boats. Never, never..."

three

Beyond the Wherry Yacht Charter, the river passes between a real mish-mash of marine and architectural styles. Boatyards are almost of necessity unprepossessing places with their sheds, crowded dykes, weed-festooned slipways, cranes and pumping-out equipment; yet even the shabbiest has a certain animated cheerfulness. But there is surely no excuse for the succession of decaying chalets and floating caravans that infest long stretches of the banks.

There are some fine thatched and stilted houses, too, but not enough to relieve the nasty taste in my mouth as I paddled downstream towards Wroxham Broad. The one consolation was that some of the most ghastly eyesores have been earmarked for demolition to make way for new developments. The danger, of course, is that these replacements could turn out to be only more permanent eyesores, a sort of suburban blight imposed on these lovely water margins.

Wroxham Broad is a splendid piece of water. If its namesake town is the capital of tourism in the Broads, then this 450 by 250-yard space is the sailing capital, for it is one of the few large sheets of open, windswept water on the upper reaches of the by-and-large tree-lined Bure. The broad has full public access even though it is privately owned and retains much of the area's formative wildness because its banks are almost devoid of buildings. The only real intrusion is its sailing clubhouse, which looks like an escapee from Legoland.

A narrow strip of carr separates the broad from the river with an entrance at each end. Ghost-hunters claim the northerly of the two is one of the region's most spectacularly haunted spots: The spectre of a Roman soldier is seen to order onlookers to make way for a phantom troop of legionaries, gladiators, horses and chariots bound for the arena, presumbly at the old imperial capital of Venta Icenorum just a few miles away outside Norwich. This ghostly display, worthy of some ectoplasmic Cecil B de Mille, is alleged to be staged regularly between April 13 and October 9.

It is roughly at this point that tide tables come into play. Catch a rising tide and a canoe trip to Hoveton Great Broad, which takes only a few minutes on the ebb, can become a half-hour ordeal by combat. And, of course, the further downstream one goes, the tougher it gets. Happily, I had taken the precaution of checking before starting out and paddled lazily to the mooring on a strip of land that separates Hoveton Great Broad from the Bure.

The broad makes its Wroxham counterpart look like a pond. It was dug out for peat between 850AD and 1350 and covers some 76 acres to a depth of only three feet, although at its unsilted peak in the mid-19th century it spanned as much as 130 acres and was ten feet deep. Today it is a wildlife reserve, managed by English Nature, and a kind of living laboratory for scientists fighting the good fight against eutrophication. I tied up my canoe at the staithe - the only way to reach the broad - and strolled along the boardwalk around Larkbush Island, a piece of virgin peat-carpeted carr that smouldered and steamed in the unseasonable warmth. The path led me through swamps that are one of a handful of locations where you can still see the painfully rare brown hawker dragonfly - the Norfolk aeshna - and emerged at the reed-fringed edge of the broad. A hide overlooks a raucous colony of common terns nesting on a platform built among the post-marked labyrinth of underwater divisions laid out by biologists who come here from as far away as Holland.

The broad, along with its smaller neighbour Hoveton Little (or Black Horse) Broad, is part of the Hoveton House estate owned by

Sir John Blofeld, a senior judge whose forefathers founded one of Broadland's oldest and most influential dynasties. Sir John, whose younger brother Henry is the BBC Test Match Special radio commentator known throughout the cricketing world as Blowers, was born and raised here and has seen many of the more dramatic events of the post-war years. Few can have been more momentous than those of March 1949 when the holiday baron Herbert Woods led a wherry, a houseboat and a flotilla of small craft to assert ancient rights of waterway on Black Horse Broad. Tom Blofeld, Sir John's father, had blocked it with 30 wooden piles; but the armada ripped them out and sailed in.

The confrontation symbolises the uneasy relationship that has always existed among landowners and tenants - not just in Norfolk, either, although ancient navigation rights add an additional layer of potential conflict to the problem. There are still plenty of privately-owned broads in the area, many of them dredged and cleared at taxpayers' expense. One local activist, who had best remain nameless, even took the unreconstructed Stalinist view that all land in the Broads should be nationalised and all waterways opened up to the public.

This is not a view shared, however, by Sir John. His two broads remain in his family although both are managed by English Nature and are freely accessible to scientists studying Broadland eco-systems. Furthermore, as part of the compromise worked out between Tom Blofeld and Herbert Woods, Black Horse is open for part of the year, nowadays to an ever-increasing number of holiday boats.

It is in this area - tourism - that Sir John has seen the greatest changes. "When I was a child," he said, "I remember seeing very, very few boats, especially motorboats. In fact, there was virtually no motorised transport at all so the area was very much quieter." This was a boon for wildlife; otters and bitterns, now such a rarity, were commonplace and the Blofeld brothers grew up with a strong awareness of the natural wonders surrounding them. Boating and fishing were part of daily life. Sir John recalled: "I used to do a lot of pike-fishing, particularly during the war when we caught them to supplement our rations."

His father farmed the estate using horse-drawn ploughs. He could also afford to pay two full-time marshmen. Sir John said: "It was a working farm and did not bring in a great deal of money. But wages were low so it was economical to cut even small amounts of reed and sedge; and alders were cut to be used as pit-props. These jobs were done by people who would probably be on the dole today." It was a self-sufficient world: "The broads provided local people with everything they needed - fish for their diets, reeds for thatching, for example. The problem now is twofold. First, there is a massive growth in population, with 12 per cent forecast in the next 15 years; and second, the changing patterns in the leisure industry bring more and more holidaymakers here in boats that create more and more disturbance."

The bete noire is phosphate-rich deposits in the mud of the riverbeds. "Motorboats keep the top of the mud in a state of permanent suspension and plants cannot get their roots down. Speed limits have helped preserve the banks but they have not helped the beds at all so eutrophication will not go away. The conservationists say they know what they are doing, but they don't really because no one has ever done this kind of work before. They are pumping out the enriched mud but they leave the water too deep for plants and create a risk of banks being undercut by the water which causes trees to fall, making shallow lagoons that put even more mud into the water."

This dredging work is being carried out in the main by the Broads Authority, which Sir John concedes has an almost impossible task to perform in keeping its various factions united. "I don't criticise their motives," he said. "The balance between democracy and efficiency is very difficult. But it is a two-headed beast. One wants to help tourism but the other, smaller, head wants conservation. The trouble is that conservation and people can negate each other."

So what is the solution? "There is only one radical answer - to shut up the broads and leave them for 50 years. That is clearly not going to happen, however. Rule by committee means an anodyne solution and the future is an uneasy compromise between commercial and conservation interests. But at least the Broads Authority is doing something."

Sir John's preferred compromise is to bar most of the broads to motorboats, which would each be equipped with a dinghy for those wishing to explore further. He would also like the broads and rivers above such barriers as Wroxham and Potter Heigham bridges to be open only to sail and manually-powered boats. He wants, too, more efficient policing: at the time of my visit, two inspectors' launches covered the whole Bure valley.

He said: "You have to have an established tourist trade because so many jobs rely on it, so the only other answer is to limit things and to look at new ideas such as electric boats. The Broads also need more money and most of the changes we will see, such as piling, will only be cosmetic because of that. The broads are silting up. But relationships between the interested parties are better today than before, although there are still too many fingers in the pie and conservation groups are too fragmented. But we may see some changes there. As for the so-called good old days, whether or not they were perfect does not matter; they have gone for ever. That's a fact of life - it is neither good nor bad. The broads will survive in the short-term but they are silting up and all the work is really like doing a King Cnut because nature will win in the end."

The same view is held across the river by Rick Southwood, manager of the English Nature reserves along the Bure. Rick, a Mancunian who came to Norfolk as a teenage student and stayed, has been working around these marshes since 1978 when he signed on as an estate worker in Woodbastwick. "I'm very worried about rising sea levels and increasing global warming," he said as we strolled across the wild open fen that he and his team have reclaimed from the sallow scrub that threatens to engulf so much of Broadland's wild places. "Something must be done - and quickly. In the short term, I am

Rick Southwood

not worried about the future of the Broads because the aquatics are getting better and so are the dykes. But as for the global outlook..." His voice trails off and he shakes his head.

But Rick - indeed, all the wardens I met - is nothing if not pragmatic and pursues, relentlessly and sometimes in the face of public anxieties, his policies of trying to restore his beloved marshes to something rather nearer their pristine state than has been seen for at least two generations.

He led me round the Woodbastwick area of his jurisdiction, Latin names tripping off his tongue with Bellamyesque facility, a man truly at one with his environment and with his belief in his work. Under a blazing May sun, we strolled through the biggest alder carr in western Europe, wandered across open fen and hay meadows and squelched carefully over peat-rich hover that floats on a cistern of suffocating mud just a few inches below the surface. But although a walk across the reserve is a sometimes alarming experience, particularly when crossing hover, the area is a rich source of eco-friendly resources that Rick believes could be harvested to give long-term sustainable management.

The fens are grazed and, with the shrubs, cut every four to ten years. This produces a twofold bonus. First, it encourages growth that in turn attracts many rarities: orchids, marsh pea, milk parsley - and, therefore, the swallowtail butterfly caterpillars that feed on it - spearwort and the rare buckler fern, wintering bitterns and eighteen kinds of dragonfly, including the aeshna. Second, the detritus can be used instead of fossil fuel when mixed with turkey litter. It is currently used by a power station just over the border at Eye in Suffolk. "But there really should be one in the Broads," said Rick.

Scrub clearance is achieved by hard graft and with the help of grazing animals. But this latter is beset with problems. In Holland, which has wetlands similar to those of Broadland, the authorities have introduced sturdy Hex cattle, wild boar, red deer and konik ponies, semi-feral horses from Poland that eat wood because they require cellulose in their diet. "One trouble is, " said Rick, "the Dutch leave them wild. The ponies have no veterinary care and when they die, their carcasses are left to rot on the ground, which is good for all scavenging creatures but would cause outrage here and we wouldn't do it.. We have had koniks here, on private land, and we are experimenting with old breeds of cattle. We also have wild red deer and there are about a hundred Chinese water deer, although they are so small and secretive we hardly ever see them." Right on cue, I spotted one in a dyke. But it was dead, the bloated victim of the ice that encrusts the backwaters of the Broads in the depths of winter.

The entire reserve, which skirts the south bank of the Bure for several miles, is dammed off from the river because of the poor water quality. "It will be a happy day when I can take down the dams," he said. But the water on the marshes is in good nick. "We have had pike breeding on the fen and we get a terrific range of insects." Entomology is just one of the panoply of skills that all reserve wardens need, although Rick finds little time for pursuing it. "There is a sad lack of great amateurs," he said, "but there are still a few around. Our moth surveys are done by local enthusiasts because I have neither the time nor their expertise. They are amazing people - they know so much."

Changing opinions mean an ever-changing approach to management. "Woods were coppiced for many years because it was thought that was the best way of keeping them healthy," Rick said, "but in recent years the experts have done a U-turn and decided that leaving fallen deadwood on the ground is better, so we do that now. There is a general problem in the Broads with short-termism, which is the curse of the age, but I try to take the long view about conservation. The truth is, our best hope is to educate - particularly people of my generation. Youngsters have a good grasp of the difficulties; it's older people who have the power who can be the problem. There is far too much sentimentalism and nostalgia."

The southern part of Rick's manor extends roughly between Salhouse and Ranworth broads. Although the river water quality is suspect, this stretch of the Bure is easy on the eye. Salhouse has two broads, although Little Broad is barely more than a pool. Salhouse Broad itself is a narrow strip of water separated from the river, like its larger neighbour Wroxham, by a carr spit. Chronic bank erosion exposed the roots of a fine old shoreline oak so badly that the tree had to be taken down for safety reasons. Nearby, the rotting hulk of what looks like a wherry yacht lies half-submerged with a tree growing through its ribs. GC Davies, a Norwich lawyer whose writings about the Broads paved the way for the tourist industry, said of Salhouse in 1883 that it offered "quiet idyllic enjoyment and rational healthy recreation...a firmer tone to body and soul for the labour of the ensuing weeks."

The Bure is fringed with carr on the run-up to the tight right-hand bend that takes boaters into Horning. The glazed top of Dydler's Mill dominates as you approach the turn; it must offer wonderful views back towards Salhouse. As I paddled along, brimstone butterflies were everywhere, fluttering among crowds of white-fronted, brent, Canada and Egyptian geese, mute and black swans, dabchicks and a host of ducks - mallard, tufted, sheldrakes, carolina and gadwall. A heron, hunting silently in the reed rond, suddenly lifted off and flew within inches of the cockpit of a passing cruiser; its occupants did not even notice. A coot chased off a duck that had strayed too close to her nest, then pursued my canoe issuing its warning call that sound horribly like a dentist's drill. Great-crested grebes ducked and dived; a month later they would be out on the water with their young riding on their backs. The orange-blue streak of a kingfisher flashed across my bows, dispersing a vast swarm of flies that hung over the water.

Horning is a pretty riparian village of old cottages, three pubs, a string of boatbuilders' sheds and an often unsightly collection of moorings and houseboats - although the numbers seem to be falling. The village contains traces of Roman occupation and was once famous for its maltings: ships biscuits for the Royal Navy were made here during the Crimean War.

But today tourism is its raison d'etre. If Wroxham is the tourism capital of the Broads, then Horning is its nostalgia capital, for it was here that Arthur Ransome's Coot Club was based. I was one of millions of children who grew up spellbound by the adventures of Tom Dudgeon, the Horning doctor's son, his proto-conservationist comrades Dick and Dorothea Callum and the boatbuilders' sons Joe, Bill and Pete - better known as the Death and Glories. Theirs was a magical world of eternal summer, moonlight escapades, carefree days, ginger beer and innocence. It is still sometimes possible to recapture that old spirit, drifting in a silence broken only by the song of reed buntings and willow tits and the lambent water lapping along the hull, cut off from the real world by alder and reed. But on the Bure, it is to be found only off the main river in a small boat.

Leaving the village centre, we pass the Ferry Inn whence a ferry has operated for a thousand years. Today, a summertime foot service links the village and Woodbastwick Staithe where, on a bitter January morning, I once found a posse of anglers fishing from the front seats of their heated cars. The inn was the scene of one of Broadland's greatest tragedies. In 1941, when local boatbuilders had turned their skills to producing motor torpedo boats for the war effort, a German bomb scored a direct hit on the pub, killing 21 people and leaving dozens more grievously hurt. The inn was later rebuilt but, in 1965, its thatch caught fire and the building was gutted. It has since been rebuilt again, this time with a tiled roof.

The entrance to Cockshoot Broad follows on the right. You can walk there from Woodbastwick Staithe or, if waterborne, tie up by the dammed entrance. A boardwalk follows the lily-clad dyke through the reeds and carr to a hide overlooking the broad itself, the first to be restored by the Broads Authority. Some 40,000 cubic metres of mud were pumped out of the water and more than 10,000 plants transplanted. Later, 700,000 fish were removed and put into the Bure to give water fleas an unthreatened feast to rid the water of its asphyxiating algae. Today the broad is the paradigm of peace, long and narrow, rich in birds, stretching towards Woodbastwick, a pretty, half-timbered estate village built for his workers by the local landowner in the 18th century. The medieval thatched church of Ss Fabian and Sebastian is the only church in England so named.

Back on the river, Horning church stands on a rise on the left flanked by a magnificent Georgian rectory. St Benedict's dates back to the 13th century and has intricate carved bench-ends. It has only one aisle - the other was pulled down in the 1750s by parishioners who sold the stone to pay for a new roof.

The dyke to Ranworth leads off from the right just beyond. The town is famous for St Helen's church, which justly enjoys the sobriquet "the Cathedral of the Broads". It not only has one of the greatest views in Broadland - 15 miles in places - for those who can face the 80-odd steps and ladders of its winding spiral stairway to the roof of the tower, it is also one of the greatest treasure-houses to be found anywhere in Britain. The pride of its collection is a truly fabulous 15th century screen painted with images of the saints and apostles. It is faded and cracked and was defaced by Puritan vandals in the 17th century but remains stunning, especially as it is set among plain whitewashed walls. How long these remain plain, however, is a matter of debate, for medieval frescoes have been discovered hidden behind part of the wash and may be extensive. St Helen's also boasts what is known as the Sarum Antiphoner, an illuminated psalter dating back to about 1400.

Ranworth has two broads - the one eponymous, the other called Malthouse. The former has been owned by the Norfolk Wildlife Trust since 1949 when it was bequeathed by Colonel Henry Cator. The broad is closed to boats and has a floating conservation centre reached by a boardwalk from a lane next to the church. Wrecked wherries were used to shore up the banks and several more, as elsewhere in the area, were sunk in the middle of the broad to prevent enemy seaplanes landing during the war. On a hot day, the walk to the conservation centre is like a hike through a tropical swamp. The reeds and rushes tower above you and the muddy ground, choked with sedge and a dazzling display of wild flowers, gives off an exhilarating stench of fecund decay. The sedge from Ranworth, cut for ridges on thatched roofs, is so prized that thatchers are said to be able to smell it.

Malthouse, by contrast, is an overworked piece of water, almost invariably chockablock with boats in the season. This is no surprise: St Helen's and the conservation centre are not the only draws, for the staithe is an attractive collection of old maltings, now converted into a shop, restaurant and information centre, and a pleasant pub, The Maltsters.

In an area noted for its ghosts, Ranworth has a good 'un. On New Year's Eve 1770, the hard-drinking squire, Colonel Thomas Sidney, challenged a neighbour to a horse race. When the colonel's mount began to flag, he shot his rival's horse, killing both the animal and its unhappy rider, who broke his neck as he fell. That night, during a party, the Master of the Wild Hunt arrived astride a fiery-nostrilled steed at Sidney's door and called him out, slinging the caddish colonel across the saddle and galloping away over the broad in a cloud of steam.

four

The mouth of the Ant, strangely enough called Antmouth, is just beyond the dyke to Ranworth. Originally, the Ant is thought to have flowed north of St Benet's Abbey into the Thurne. A causeway once linked the abbey and Horning Hall but at some date the river was diverted into the Bure and the causeway cut.

St Benet's has few remains: desultory foundations and an arch opening on to an 18th century mill, putatively the oldest brick-built mill in the county. St Benet's is the only medieval monastery in Britain whose ruin cannot be blamed on the iconoclastic Henry VIII. The house, founded in Saxon days, razed with customary violence by the Vikings and refounded in 1020 by King Cnut, was

Eric Edwards

the sole survivor of the Dissolution of 1536, when it was combined with the Bishopric of Norwich. The Bishop is still Abbot of St Benet's and makes a riverborne pilgrimage to the abbey every August to hold an outdoor service. At its peak, St Benet's owned property in 76 parishes and was incredibly wealthy, not least from turbary rights. A million turves of peat were dug each year from the Hoveton area alone in the Middle Ages. The abbey's benefactors included Shakespeare's great comic hero Sir John Falstaff, who is buried here. But royal clemency could not save St Benet's. Within a decade of the Dissolution, it closed because there were not enough brothers to sustain it and it fell quickly into ruin.

The first thing one notices about the Ant is how narrow it is, at times being little wider than the beam of two cruisers. Come summer, it can resemble a motorway tailback rather than a river. Its problem is that it is too pretty, meandering through marshes studded with mills and old farmhouses and, later on, with woodland. It is also the only route to Barton Broad. Canoeing is a perilous pasttime here, for the wash from boats, although largely absorbed by the reed rond, is apt to swill over the bows. I was nearly swamped one August morning when some moron in a cruiser tried to shoot Ludham's arched bridge at full throttle and crunched into the stonework. It took all my effort not to laugh out loud at his misfortune.

Despite the congestion, the stretch from the bridge to How Hill is one of my favourite pieces of water in Broadland. Turf Fen, with its double-scooped mill, glitters on the left while How Hill, a gorgeous Edwardian thatched mansion, stands on a rise 40ft above sea level, the highest point in the national park. I tied up at the staithe and walked to Toad Hole cottage, an old eelman's home preserved by the Broads Authority. It is tiny and extraordinarily snug. The grounds of How Hill - the house is now a trust-run environmental education centre - contain a nature trail that leads to Crome's Broad, an idyllic jungle-rimmed lake where kingfishers dart and shoals of roach cavort covertly in the shallows. The bosky grounds also contain a rather macabre souvenir, Hitler's Oak, given to the yachtsman Chris Boardman, whose family owned the house, after he won a gold medal at the 1936 Berlin Olympics.

How Hill is the base of one of Broadland's most famous characters, Eric Edwards, a marshman for more than 30 years who is as well known for his media appearances as for his astonishing craftsmanship. I ran into Eric as he worked with a neighbouring marshman, Andy Hewitt, on a freezing cold yet brilliantly sunlit and windless January day when the marshes sparkled with frost and the river was utterly still. I had deliberately not tried to interview Eric simply because he is so well-known locally and I was preoccupied with "unsung" Broadlanders. But fate had obviously decreed otherwise and he chatted enthusiastically about his love of the marshes in his care. He had just unloaded 1,000 shooves of cut reed on the staithe from his quanted lighter. This ringe of reed, as he called it, stood like a golden wall in the dazzling afternoon; and as we chatted, Eric kept glancing at it like a father keeping an eye on his child. "You won't see anything like this very often," he said with a mixture of pride and sadness. By a curious coincidence, the Aldred brothers, who feature later in this chapter, arrived at this point to collect some of Eric's reed. But what should have been a great photo-opportunity became instead a cause of much mirth photographer David Koppel and I - London greenhorns both - battled to control Eric's boat and keep our balance as we looked for an angle from which to picture the four locals on the staithe.

Back on the river, a grass snake swam oscillatingly across my bows as a lapwing dive-bombed a hissing heron hunting too close to its nest. Two unique mills stand on the bank here: Clayrack, a 17th century hollow-post that was moved from Ranworth, and Boardman's, a skeleton tower trestle.

A gentle paddle further on, I reached Irstead. This is a classic Broadland village, a riverside collection of old red-brick cottages mingling with thatched and sometimes stilted houses set in willow-shaded gardens. It is worth mooring at the staithe and strolling up to St Michael's church, which has a painted screen and a 600-year-old carved font, before walking to Irstead Manor, a 17th century thatched mansion a few minutes along the Neatishead road. The garden has a 6th century AD Justinian capital, presumably picked up on some Georgian Grand Tour.

Irstead is the gateway to Barton Broad, a 170-acre lake that provides some of the best sailing in the region; so good, in fact, that the boy Horatio Nelson learned the art here in the 18th century. The broad, which is owned by the NWT, has been undergoing a £1.5million restoration masterminded by the Broads Authority with money provided by the National Lottery's Millennium Commission. Some of the cash is being used to resurrect Pleasure Hill Island (created, so the story goes, from ballast dumped by wherrymen) to its former glory. When I saw it, it was nothing more than a few trees clinging precariously to its eroded and now submerged soil. Out on the broad, common and black terns pirouetted through the air inches above the surface and a score of dinghies, crewed mainly by children, scudded across the water with masts almost touching the waves. Dredgers were working in the centre of the broad. The mud they remove is dumped in terraces that resemble paddy fields in the grounds of Barton Hall, a 1745 house owned by Jonathan Peel, past chairman of the Broads Authority. The latest mud, heavily eutrophied, is placed on the highest step, from where the water seeps, being naturally filtered on the way, until it runs, clean and nutrient-free, back into the broad.

First left off the broad takes you into Limekiln Dyke, which leads to Neatishead, a village whose centre is a street of old cottages, the White Horse pub, a shop/post office and a couple of bed and breakfast establishments, including Ye Olde Saddlery, run by the redoubtable Mrs Thompson and the base for most of my travels in northern Broadland. Neatishead has a small RAF base that is part of Strike Command's defence network. Although it does not appear on my Ordnance Survey map, the Ministry of Defence was quick to assure me that it is not part of some Secret Squirrel operation. The village has two staithes - the public one near the post office and a second belonging to the

Barton Angler, a cosy hotel five minutes by foot along the Irstead road.

Nearby, a short hop by road, is Beeston St Lawrence, a living example of the power landowners once wielded. A local squire decided the houses of his tenants marred his view of the church - so he pulled down the village and rebuilt it elsewhere. The church is interesting, too, for a V2 rocket came down nearby in 1945, blowing the parapet from the tower and shattering all the church's 18th century glass. Another short diversion, 20 minutes' walk by public footpath over the fields, leads to Alderfen Broad, a small but pretty landlocked piece of water with a pleasant woodland walk.

The second turning on the left on Barton Broad leads to the grassed staithe of Barton Turf, a village with many Georgian cottages and a church, St Michael's, which is said to have a painted screen second only to Ranworth's. I say "said to have" because I was unable to see it; a churchwarden's notice on the porch explained with poignant brevity that the door was kept locked because so many treasures had been filched.

On the opposite side of the broad lie the dykes that lead to Sutton and Stalham. Sutton used to have its own huge broad - the ring of mature trees give an indication of its former size - but it is now overgrown with reeds. The staithe is a bit of a stew of mainly private moorings dominated by a hotel but the view across the reedy savannah from the path that follows the dyke is tremendous. I met an angler walking his dog who, though a Broadlander born and bred, broke the mould of the traditional huntin', shootin' and fishin' countryman by complaining that something should be done about the number of ichthyophagous cormorants, not because they were cheating him out of his quarry but because they were causing grebes and kingfishers to go hungry. His eyes lit up when he described watching the mating dance of grebes. He also said the water had been clearer since the dyke froze over the previous January. Could a gargantuan deep freeze be the answer to Broadland pollution?

Stalham is a bustling market town. The church that lies at its heart is said to be connected to the Maids Head Inn by a secret tunnel dug to keep drunken ecclesiastical builders out of the sight of prim burghers. Stalham Hall, a five-bayed, 17th century edifice with a double porch containing a Stuart sundial, is singled out by Pevsner as "remarkable and charming"; the latter adjective could equally apply to the town, which was sometime home to the prolific 20th century composer EJ Moeran.

Stalham is cut off from its staithe by a main road; it is tempting to think this is because the town is ashamed of its waterfront. I certainly could not blame it. Apart from a Georgian wherry granary and a handful of old cottages, it is a bit of a dump, overwhelmed by a boatyard - the biggest in the Broads - with all its paraphenalia of ugly sheds and quays. It's easy to forget, of course, that it provides vitally-needed jobs, but I cannot accept that lucre and looks are so mutually exclusive.

A mile or so away stands nine-storey Sutton Mill, reputedly the tallest corn mill in Britain, built in 1789, rebuilt in 1859 after a

Chris Nunn

fire, last used commercially in 1940 and now run by a remarkable man called Chris Nunn who, since the death of his wife in 1994, has been trying to restore it single-handedly. He also presides over the most eclectic, not to say eccentric, museum I have ever seen, a truly amazing collection of domestic and commercial knick-knacks that include - and this merely scratches the surface - tinned food, steam-powered engines, tools, razors, boots, bikes, clothes, pre-war detergents and, as the pride of the exhibition, a complete 1880 chemist's shop transported from the Isle of Wight in the late 1980s. It also has a vast collection of pipes, tobacco, cigars and cigarettes, some made in Victorian times, that recall the 17th century Norfolk pioneer James Rolfe who was the first man to grow tobacco commercially in Virginia.

Chris had originally planned a career in hotels but was driven out by what he saw as the hypocrisy of big business. I asked him why he chose to buy a windmill. "Because I couldn't get the aqueduct I wanted in Somerset," he replied. "We bought the mill off the local farmer and we have spent the last 20 years restoring it. It was in a terrible state when we got here and we have spent hundreds of thousands on the mill and museum over the years. My only income comes from visitors" - up to 2,000 a year - "and since my wife died and our daughter Robyn left home, I have been going backwards. I do everything myself and all without grants."

The lack of grants in a country obsessed with its past makes his eyes blaze. "The way Lottery money is handed out is disgraceful," he said. "I love opera but the millions that went to the Royal Opera House was outrageous. People like me will never get to go there. They tell me I'm too far out of the way; but the Science Museum in London is out of the way, too, because you can't park near it. I have plenty of parking so I don't hold with that argument. We are told to conserve our heritage but we get no help to do it."

The Herculean labour of maintaining - indeed, expanding - the mill and museum goes on despite these concerns. "Money does not really matter in the end," he said, "as long as you have something to eat and a roof over your head. You can't just take, take, take like the Maxwells of this world - you have to give something back. This is my something."

I asked if he would ever sell his museum collection to raise cash. He looked daggers, as if I had suggested selling a child. "I could never, ever do that. I started this 37 years ago and it just sort of ballooned. I could never part with it."

I climbed the winding stair, past a sign reading "Please! Do Not Hit Our Wood With Your Head", to the top of the mill. The view is better even than that from the tower of St Helen's at Ranworth. I counted 20 churches, two lighthouses and at least 12 mills; I could also see Horsey Mere and Hickling Broad and, more distant still, the silver shimmer of the North Sea. Before going back to work, Chris told me: "There is still a huge amount to do. It's just a shame I won't be around to see it finished."

Saddened, I paddled away from Barton Broad up the now tree-lined, meandering Ant towards Wayford Bridge. On the right is Hunsett's Mill, a small tower beside a lovely cottage in a flower-festooned garden that is

Mike and Steve Aldred

the classic picture-postcard spot in all Broadland. Wayford Bridge was built at the site of an ancient ford and Roman camp. Tyler's Cut leads off from the left to Dilham while the Ant itself becomes the Dilham and North Walsham canal, closed to large boats but accessible for smaller craft towards East Ruston and Honing.

East Ruston was once home to a remarkable scholar, Richard Porson. Born the son of the parish clerk in 1759, he was a child of precocious and prodigious talent. Despite his humble background, he won places at Eton and Trinity College, Cambridge, and became Regius Professor of Greek at Cambridge when he was only 33. The village is also home to master craftsmen Steve and Michael Aldred and Bill Cordaroy.

The Aldred brothers are two of Norfolk's most sought-after thatchers; they are also living examples of heredity. Their father is a thatcher, living at Sutton, and both of them grew up with the smell of reed and sedge in their nostrils. But neither had planned to follow in his footsteps until destiny took a hand - and both discovered, though they would be too modest to admit it, that they had a genius for this most ancient craft. I joined them for an afternoon as they wove their magic on a farmhouse roof. Steve, bearded and swarthy, is the older of the two. He started off with ambitions to farm but, having been made redundant, went to work with his dad for four years. "I was learning the trade," he said. Trade? Watching them at work, "art" would seem a more apposite term. Steve set up on his own in 1981 and was joined five years later by his brother. They look like chalk and cheese - Michael is fair, clean-shaven and bespectacled - but they have a shared passion for their craft and a shared enthusiasm for its traditions. While many thatchers are turning to cheaper foreign imports, the brothers remain loyal to Phragmites communis, Norfolk reed, once universally renowned as the Prince of Thatch. "We know the reedcutters and we know their jobs depend on it," said Steve. "Norfolk reed used to be the best in the world, although pollution may affect it now."

Eutrophication again... But although the brothers acknowledge the problems of nutrient enrichment, they do not believe it is the only cause. Steve recalled: "When I used to sail on Hickling Broad in the early 60s I often fell in and clearly remember seeing the weeds at the bottom and all the fish. Then they dredged out a channel on the broad; but they dug it too deep and all this peaty stuff came up and made the water murky. Part of the trouble now is that reedbeds are not managed like they once were. Reed litter is not cleared out so nitrates get caught in the beds and that affects the quality of the reed. It's not as good as it was, say, twenty years ago."

How, I wondered, will that affect their work? "It's hard to tell," Steve replied. "A thatch should last between fifty and seventy years so it's too early to say whether a roof will have a shorter life." And is the answer more cash for restoration? Steve shook his head. "There is a huge amount of money being poured into the Broads but a lot of it is wasted on unnecessary bureaucracy and on jobs that shouldn't exist. They should just employ a load of marshmen to work round the year; that would do more good."

The Aldred brothers

Bill Cordaroy and Jason Greenberry

Reed is Steve and Michael's chief medium. Bundles, each covering a square foot, are laid in layers on the roof and then ridged with sedge, which is more pliable. The ridge is seamed with hazel wands in a pattern that is unique to each thatcher and is said to be as distinctive as a fingerprint. I pointed to a thatch on the house next door and asked Steve to name its creator. He did - although he later admitted with a chuckle that he had watched the thatcher do it.

The brothers spend much of their time on houses and barns but they have regularly undertaken altogether grander tasks. For example, they thatched the church in their neighbouring village, Brumstead. "That took us eight weeks and we used about 4,000 bundles of reeds," Steve said. "The length of time we take depends a lot on the weather. We don't get much rain in Norfolk, so we don't lose too much time that way, but it can be grim in winter when a north-easterly is blowing or there is a heavy frost. The reeds get unmanageable and the wands become brittle and snap, so we have to stop work for a time. Fortunately, we have plenty of work on so we don't need to worry at the moment."

There's no doubt that the brothers, who both have young families, enjoy the deep contentment born of finding their true vocation in an environment they love. The perfect illustration of this was a story Michael told about visiting a friend who left Broadland to live in Bromley, one of the more faceless of south London's suburbs. "He's lonely," Michael said. "He doesn't even know the people in his block of flats, let alone in his street. He comes back here just to talk to people. I spent two days with him in London and that was enough for me. The people there were like an ant army, everybody in suits marching along and wrapped up in themselves."

Ironically, many of the Aldreds' clients these days are townies with second homes in Norfolk. But Steve said: "I don't mind that because it puts money into the local economy, although it's tough on youngsters who can no longer afford to live in the villages because it pushes up house prices." These same townies are also an increasingly powerful pressure group for the conservation lobby. "The trouble is," Steve said, "they don't understand the countryside. Good management of the countryside doesn't always make it look pretty. The biggest waste of money at the moment is the attempt to save the bittern. Bitterns were extinct in the Broads a hundred years ago - it's just part of the natural cycle. What you have to remember is that the Broads are man-made so it's not a question of preserving them in their 'natural' state. Then there's hunting... but I bet you'll find more wildlife on a well-run shooting estate than anywhere else. Don't ban hunting. If you don't like it, don't do it; but don't tell other people what to do."

A thatch is not cheap but demand is growing. "We're always busy," Steve said, "although some customers make me laugh because they say I'm a skilled craftsman or artist then quibble about every penny. What we have to worry about now is how badly pollution has affected the reeds. But I am an optimist. I think the Broads have turned a corner, not the corner; but it will happen because it's in everybody's interest."

Meanwhile, the brothers' ambition is to carry on for as long as they can, making hay while the sun shines, so to speak. With burgeoning order books, it is hard to say what could stop them - except an accident. Steve has already twice fallen off roofs, although without serious injury. "But I wouldn't want to do anything else," he said. I assume he meant the thatching, not the roof-diving...

A gate in Steve's garden was made by his fellow East Ruston master craftsman, Bill Cordaroy, member of the Worshipful Company of Blacksmiths and another man who has found his true vocation. Unlike the Aldreds, he is not a Broadlander by birth - but he is one by inclination. He moved to the village in the late 1970s after working as an engineer in Cambridge, buying an old council farmhouse for £10,000 with his wife Jan, building his own forge and workshop and renovating the cottage from scratch. He is assisted by Jason Greenberry, a talented blacksmith who joined him in 1984.

"I came here to escape the rat-race," Bill said as he showed me round the forge, the walls lined with the tools of his trade which he had either made himself or bought at antique sales. "They're lovely, aren't they?" he asked with unselfconscious pride. If the tools were lovely, his work was gorgeous. The workshop was scattered with a cross-section of his peerless output, creations in iron, steel, brass or aluminium that range from simple thatching pins to spiral staircases, doorknobs to garden statues, hinges to lamp-posts, nails to an extraordinary hollow sphere that would soon hang as a candelabra inside Norwich Cathedral. And gates, numberless gates, including a half-ton pair

Bill Cordaroy

in the front garden waiting to be set up at the entrance to a house in East Ruston once the owner's trees have grown to the correct height. "They took Jason and me four months," Bill said. "We do a lot of gates."

Bill came to Norfolk hoping never again to have to use an arc-welder and dreaming of producing contemporary work of his own design. "The first just hasn't happened because I have to earn a living," he said without a trace of bitterness, "and I don't have time to do much of the second. But I love the work and I like the pace of life here. The business has really taken off and there are plenty of commissions around."

Bill's first major commission - and the one that made his name - was a pair of gates for the chapel at St John's College, Cambridge. "They took me nine months and I only charged them £4,000. I got the estimate badly wrong and they got a great deal. But it led to other things, so I'm not complaining."

Those "other things" included commissions from such contrasting institutions as the multinational pharmaceuticals company Glaxo and St Alban's Abbey, both in Hertfordshire, grilles for the ruins of St Benet's Abbey, railings for a pyramidic mausoleum at Blickling Hall in north Norfolk and nails for the medieval barn just a few miles down the road at Waxham (of which more later), along with thousands of less glamorous orders worth only a few pounds a time. Bill said: "I like the small jobs like thatching pins because it keeps me at the anvil. Blacksmiths need to work on the anvil but many of them don't."

Optical skills are just as important as manual skills. "I do all my designs freehand," he said, "so you have to have a good eye, particularly when doing an original piece." One of these latter is a sculpture called The Paper Woman, a faceless wonder that has been widely exhibited. He has also contributed to a steel tree being crafted by blacksmiths from around the world to stand in the Polish port of Gdansk, birthplace of Solidarity, and made a prize-winning contribution to a 30ft-tall waterside monument in Newcastle upon Tyne called The Blacksmiths' Needle. The theme of the sculpture is the senses and Bill's piece is entitled "Perspective".

Over a pub lunch , he enthused about the community of blacksmiths that recognises no political boundaries. "The Gdansk tree is just one example," he said. "I visited Estonia before the Russians left and made friends with craftsmen there. We've been back twice since. It was wonderful that first trip, like walking back in time. But it is already changing now that it is independent." He and Jan were preparing for a month's visit to India. "It's not a bad life, is it?" he smiled.

five

Assuming you don't misread the tides, Antmouth to the river Thurne is a short paddle, although often perilously busy in summer. I have never managed this stretch in the season without getting soaked from bouncing off the wash of cruisers.

On the right bank of the Bure between these two estuaries lies Fleet Dyke, the entrance to South Walsham's two broads. The outer one is a popular spot with a floating pizza house usually anchored in the middle and a small shop on the staithe. The houses that surround it are among the loveliest in Broadland, a mixture of red brick and whitewash, half-timbering and thatch - and now worth a packet. John Atkins, a leading light of the Broads Society, lives in one that his great-grandfather bought just after the First World War for a few hundred pounds. The beauty of the setting means that today the house is worth a small fortune; but back then, it was considered terribly infra dig to live by the water. John's mother, 92 when I met her, said her family did not want to move there and her grandma, the original buyer's wife, loathed it. How times change...

The inner broad was once part of the South Walsham Hall estate. The house is now an upmarket hotel and country club while 170 acres of the garden are run by the Fairhaven Trust. Its rhododendrons are magnificent in May; but even when they are not in bloom, a walk through the dense, often dripping, growth is an enthralling experience: vast Gunneria gigantica overwhelm the banks of the labyrinthine dykes, multicoloured lilies and other waterside plants cluster round the towering trees, one of which is an oak that was a sapling when William the Conqueror was trying to capture Hereward the Wake in the fens at Ely.

The inner broad itself was the scene of one of the more ludicrous confrontations between plebian and patrician. On Whit Monday, 1901, the owner wired off the water and moored his houseboat, The Ark, beside the entrance. A crowd of angry locals gathered on the staithe. Unfortunately, one or two of them seem to have been the worse for drink and mistook The Ark's firepump and polished brass telescope for some species of machine-gun - with the result that panic set in. Eventually, the truth was revealed and a compromise reached: access to the broad was granted but swimming, mooring, fishing and landing rights were denied. These proscriptions are still in force today.

South Walsham village contains an ecclesiastical curiosity: two churches in one graveyard. Legend has it that two sisters wanted to build a house of worship but were unable to agree a plan, so St Lawrence's and St Mary's were built almost back to back. The truth is rather more mundane; the churches were erected at the meeting point of two ancient manors on one of the few pieces of rising ground in the area. St Lawrence's was part-ruined in a fire in 1827 and is destined to become the village hall. St Mary's contains an inscribed stone in memory of an abbot of St Benet's; it was once used as a doorstep at the Duke of Norfolk's house in Norwich.

The Thurne is one of the oddest rivers in Broadland - in fact, in Britain - for it used to flow the other way. Nowadays it runs down through Horsey Mere and meets the Bure just beyond the village of Thurne. But only a few generations ago, it flowed from the Bure into the sea via the now blocked Hundred Stream near Horsey.

Thurne village is among the most easily recognised settlements in the region, for a pair of mills, one black, the other white, stand sentinel either side of the river by its dyke. On a rise behind the village is St Edmund's church whose tower contains a peephole offering a complete view of St Benet's across the marshes and was said to be used to hold warning lamps; as much, no doubt, to alert smugglers as monks. Thurne was once part of a low-lying estuarine island, called Flegg Isle by Norse settlers, that was joined to the mainland only in the Middle Ages when the area was drained. Indeed, the village and river are thought to take their name from a Viking warrior who made his home here.

The river is a delight for canoeing, for the tide runs nowhere near as rapidly as it does on the Bure. Womack Water opens up on the left, leading to Ludham, a village of white-washed thatched houses with a huge 15th century church, St Catherine's, whose roof supports are styled in the form of Catherine wheels. Ludham was home to the artist and author Edward Seago, 1919-74, who helped teach Prince Charles to paint. Seago painted many of the greatest figures of his day, such as the Second World War military leaders Auchinleck and Alexander and the prima ballerina Dame Alicia Markova. He also helped the RAF develop camouflage and invented an infra-red paint. Seago wrote several books in collaboration with the Poet Laureate John Masefield as well as several on his own, including Circus Company (he ran away to join the circus as a youngster) and A Canvas To Cover. Seago was the latest in a line of great Broadland artists that started with the Georgian painter John Sell Cotman; yet these artists, not to mention composers and writers from Norfolk, have been utterly overshadowed by the beatific genius of their cousins in neighbouring Suffolk: John Constable, Thomas Gainsborough, George Crabbe, Benjamin Britten. Why should this be so? No proper explanation has ever been offered.

Half an hour from Thurnemouth by canoe and the first of Potter Heigham's riparian chalets hove into view. There are more than a hundred of these holiday homes, many of them old cricket pavilions that have been variously described as "charming" and "a bungaloid slum". I veer towards the former description, mainly because they are evocative of childhood forays along the river. The bungalows have been the subject of a long - and often vitriolic - squabble between the owners and the Broads Authority, which makes no secret of its wish to wipe them from the face of the earth.

One of the pavilions' staunchest defenders is Bill Seath, a bluff Yorkshireman who came to the Broads for a week in 1967 and stayed, buying one of the bungalows and becoming well-known in local marine circles because his work as a compass adjuster took him into most of Broadland's boatyards.

Bill, a fomer Merchant Navy officer who runs a marine instruments company in Lowestoft, is a leading light of the Broads Society, which was founded in 1954 by a South Walsham builder and ex-lumberjack called Len Ramuz and a group of enthusiasts who foresaw that uncontrolled pollution and planning could destroy the waterways within a generation. A committee created by the society eventually led to the formation of the Broads Authority. Nowadays, the society's 2,000-odd members see themselves primarily as an environmental watchdog; certainly they remain an influential lobby on the local political scene.

Bill bought his bungalow as a place to moor his yacht, Green Ginger, and his motorboat, Red Pepper, and lives there with his wife Diana during the summer. The land is owned by the Environment Agency and sublet to the Broads Authority, which in the early 1980s drafted its Potter Heigham plan in which it declared its intention to raze all the bungalows south of a line drawn apparently arbitrarily across the Thurne.

Residents were initially unaware of this plan - until there was a sudden sharp rent increase. "Some of the owners went to the town hall to complain about the rises," Bill said, "and they were told 'I don't know what you are worrying about, they'll all be gone soon.' That slip of the tongue was the first anyone knew of the Broads Authority's intentions to get rid of them. What followed was a war of attrition in which common sense was not necessarily applied."

A deal was struck in 1985. Most of the properties were given new 99-year leases and 40 that had been earmarked for demolition were given 15 years. "It was a bit like the Treaty of Versailles," Bill said. "In other words, a balls-up."

It was at that point that Bill and Diana bought one of the short-lease properties, reflecting that the Broads Authority's plan was probably unenforceable legally and that even if they had to burn the house down when the lease ran out in 2001, they would have had their money's worth.

In the meantime, the tenants' association decided to try to save all the bungalows. Bill recalled: "I photographed every plot from the river and from a helicopter. Some of them were undoubtedly eyesores, so we suggested our own plan - for example, getting rid of outhouses and hedges. I went on radio and said that under the BA plan, some of the good bungalows would be pulled down while

many of the nastier ones would remain. We got offers of assistance from all over the place - even Friends of the Earth asked if they could help. Finally, at a council meeting, one member talked of 'vandalism'. It was at that point that I was convinced we were going to win."

When I talked to Bill again some months later, he and his fellow owners were celebrating because the Broads Authority had scrapped the clause requiring demolition and substituted one suggesting that owners and officials work together to improve the appearance of the riverbank. Bill said: "In other words, the authority backed down knowing full well that when it went to appeal, a planning inspector would agree with us. I am certain it was the tactic of offering an alternative proposal that won the day."

Potter Heigham is most famous for its 13th century bridge, a triple-arched stone construction with only 6' 8" of headroom: a tight squeeze for small cruisers and all but impassable for some of the more monstrous leviathans that ply these waters. It was almost unmanageable for wherrymen, too, who had to weigh down their boats with rocks until the water spilled over the decks if they wanted to shoot the central arch. But this obstacle is good news for those of us in small boats who rarely have to risk being swamped on the upper Thurne. It is good news, too, for wildlife, for the water soon becomes gin-clear above the bridge. A second span carries the by-pass over the river a few yards further upstream. It is deceptively low. One August afternoon, I and a dozen others watched a young man clamber on to the roof of his hired cruiser as it approached the bridge, his back towards it. While the rest of us stood dumbstruck, a local boatman shouted a warning. The tripper turned a nano-second before the concrete hit him chest-on with a sickening thud, sending him plummeting on to the deck from which he bounced into the water. Incredibly, he swam away with no injury - apart from the fatal one to his pride, of course.

The town's other main landmarks are the Herbert Woods tower - in fact, a water-tower disguised by faded blue weatherboarding - and Latham's, an Aladdin's Cave of a shop that is a kind of miniature Roys. On my most recent visit there, a sign at the entrance warned: "Under no circumstances may maggots be taken into the store."

There are a few bungalows above Potter but they fizzle out by the time you reach Candle Dyke, which opens up on the left and leads to Hickling and Horsey. Pressing straight on, you reach a farm's chain-link ferry connecting the marshes with a lane that leads to Martham, a twenty-minute walk away.

Martham is built round a large and attractive green. The splendid parish church of St Michael's is the burial place of the pre-Norman ascetic Walstan, Norfolk's patron saint of agriculture, who turned his back on a rich inheritance to lead the simple life. He was laid to rest in 1016, aged 55. St Michael's also contains an extraordinary memorial, dated 1730, put up by one Christopher Burraway to Alice - "my Sister, my Mistres, my Mother, and my Wife." Christopher, it seems, was the product of an incestuous union between his father and his sister. For many years he lost touch with his sister-mother and later, unwittingly, he entered her service as a steward. They fell in love and took their wedding vows. But one night in the marriage bed, Alice recognised a distinctive birthmark on Christopher and the appalling truth was revealed.

The river between Martham and its terminus at West Somerton is probably the most beautiful in all of Broadland: clear water, smaragdine underwater plants where pike hunt an unending supply of smaller fish, gleaming yellow water lilies, golden beds of swaying, susurrating reed offering tantalising glimpses of convoys of ducks and geese on the open water of Martham's two broads (both off-limits to boats), soaring marsh harriers and, as I was lucky enough to see, touring ospreys, busy dragonflies, graceful swallowtail butterflies - and all around, the eternal music of unseen reed birds which anyone in a motorboat will never hear.

The Hundred Stream, which once emptied into the sea, lies stagnantly on the left as you pass Martham Broad North, a brisk paddle from the tiny staithe at West Somerton. Just outside the village stands a wind-farm, a double row of vast turbines that hum round the clock. It is a gross offence to many; personally, I find it rather impressive.

West Somerton was the birthplace in the second decade of the 19th century of the so-called Norfolk Giant, Robert Hales. In his day, Hales was said to be the tallest man in the world. He stood 7' 8" in his stockinged feet, had a 64" chest, a 62" waist and a 7' 3" sister, Mary. He began his working life as a wherrymen and later joined the Royal Navy, from which he was discharged for being too tall. Anyone who has ever visited Nelson's flagship Victory, with its child-sized gun-deck ceilings, will readily understand why. Hales and his sister were snapped up by Phineas Barnum, the American circus showman, and went to the USA, where they were exhibited in Barnum's notorious freak show with the world's smallest man, General Tom Thumb, who, at only 25" tall, barely reached Robert's knees. Hales ended his days on the streets of Norwich, selling penny leaflets about his sad life. He died of tuberculosis and was buried in St Mary's, West Somerton. He was 43.

One day, I walked from West Somerton across the fields to Horsey Mere. I was wearing shorts and a T-shirt, for the sun was shining hotly. But after about 20 minutes, a sea-roke swept in, sending the temperature plunging and reducing visibility to no more than a few dozen yards. Shivering, I picked my way nervously through the maze of dykes in the eldritch half-light. After what seemed an age (but was probably half and hour) the insubstantial silhouette of Horsey Mill emerged from the mist. Within five minutes, the roke had dispersed and the sun beat down once more. The mill, like the mere, is owned by the National Trust and was the last to be built in Broadland, in 1912 - the same year as the last trading wherry was completed. It was a working mill until 1943 when it was struck by lightning. It has since been restored and, along with Hunsett's Mill on the Ant, is one of the most photographed buildings in the national park.

Horsey is a mile or so from the sea and was a favourite place for smugglers, particularly those trafficking tea, gin, brandy, tobacco and silk, which were once subject to harsh duties. This contraband was landed and concealed in mills, whose sails were used to flash warnings of approaching excisemen. While contraband may have provided millers with much-needed extra funds, it did nothing for their reputation. But perhaps they cared not one jot, for it was tarnished enough already: as early as the 13th century, Chaucer called his miller "a master hand at stealing".

Horsey was a favourite childhood haunt of Sir John Betjeman, one of Masefield's successors as Poet Laureate. Betjeman's father kept a boat on the Broads and, recalling those happy times, his son wrote:

How welcoming the inland reeds appear,
The wood-smoke and the breakfast and the frying,
And your warm freshwater ripples, Horsey Mere.

The propinquity of the sea means that the mere is often unnavigable in small boats - I have been swamped by waves at least 3ft high. But that same juxtaposition means that Horsey - and its neighbouring broads of Hickling and Martham - enjoy an unparalleled diversity of wildlife drawn to its brackish water. For example, the upper Thurne is home to the only breeding bitterns left in Broadland; swallowtails are more common here than anywhere else and a herd of European cranes has colonised the marshes at Horsey.

The mere has an unnerving aptitude for occasionally turning bright orange, the result of ochre, which is discussed in more detail in the next chapter. Nowhere is this problem more evident than in Waxham New Cut, a channel suitable only for small craft that runs to the village that bears its name a mile and a half away. Waxham, especially the church of St John's, seems extraordinarily remote, often beset with sea-fogs and always exuding an aura of a lost Eden. History bears this out. A large 12th century manor house once stood here, built by the Calthorpe family who gave their name to a small landlocked broad nearby that marks one of the limits of the national park. The manor was later owned by Sir Thomas Wodehouse, an Elizabethan official, who laid out a walled garden around the hall and whose simple but striking tomb stands in St John's. But the hall fell into disrepair and eventually vanished; all that remains is its 15th century gatehouse, a magnificent thatch-and-flint tithe barn 180' long and Sir Thomas's wall which, bizarrely, was decorated with Aztec motifs in cement in the 19th century. The air of desolation is completed by the knowledge that the twin village of Waxham Parva, and its church, has been lost to the sea.

The way to Hickling from Horsey Mere, which boaters are asked to stay off in the winter months, takes you down Meadow Dyke, a narrow, twisting waterway lined with tall reeds that passes on the left tiny Blackfleet Broad, less than a foot deep, and, on the right, Stubb Mill, a four-storey mill dating from the early 19th century. The mill stands at the end of a lane off which is the main entrance to the Norfolk Wildlife Trust's

Hickling reserve. Meadow Dyke finally opens out into Heigham Sound, a shallow sheet of water that links Hickling Broad to Candle Dyke and the Bure.

Veering right, I paddled out on to Hickling Broad, glad of a calm day for the broad can be just as rough as Horsey Mere - perhaps even more so, for it is many times bigger. This whole area did not exist a thousand years ago: it was part of a vast estuary fed by the Yare that contained Flegg Isle and placed the site of what is now Norwich on the shore of the North Sea.

six

Hickling was my introduction to Broadland as a 12-year-old in 1967; and it was a revelation. I was born and raised in the heart of London and my only knowledge of what lay beyond its concrete canyons was an annual foray into the countryside in the summer holidays to some of the more rugged parts of Britain - the Yorkshire Moors, Snowdonia, the Cheviots - which, though impressive, I never enjoyed other than in a superficial touristic sense. Hickling, however, was different, for I stayed with a schoolfriend whose father owned a farm on the edge of the broad and I saw, for the first time, what it was to live close to nature, to work the land at the expense of blood, sweat and blisters, to be a part of the cycle of the

David Jenkin

seasons, to treat the natural world with unsentimental respect, to experience the place without getting bogged down by the phoney idyll which I had previously perceived the countryside to be. Above all, I saw how much there was to love about this place - the reedbeds whispering and agleam; the waters of the broad coruscating in the sunshine; frost-covered rushes looking like sticks of crystallised honey; the haunting boom of an invisible bittern; a lone marsh harrier quartering the marshes; the cry of a screech-owl in the perfect silence of the night; the distant silver glint of Orion's Belt in a midnight sky whose overwhelming vastness is the especial, perhaps unique, hallmark of East Anglia's flatlands.

That first visit instilled an appreciation of Broadland - and the countryside - that has never dissipated. It also had a profound influence on my personal philosophy of life and was responsible for some of my most fundamental convictions. Foremost among these is an almost religious feeling for the beauty of our world - and for its intrinsic fragility. Gadding about the broads and rivers in a gun-punt, I was filled with a sense of wonder, still with me today, at the life-force that seemed to ooze from the very mud and soak into my consciousness. But its delicacy was brought home to me when, one day, I pulled from the water a magnificent 16lb pike that was the long-dead victim of the pollution that was already reaching epidemic proportions; on another, the boathouse dyke was choked with detergent foam at least a foot deep.

Hickling also spawned my abiding belief in the sanctity of life in all its multitudinous forms, a lesson learned in tearful horror when, for alleged sport, I took up an air rifle for the first time and shot a blackbird. The first pellet crippled it and I had to shoot a second into its head at point-blank range to put it out of its misery. The accusing look in its gold-rimmed eye haunts me still and I have never since knowingly killed any living thing - not even a fly.

There is an acute irony in this, for Hickling is one of the most famous killing grounds in the Broads. Wildfowling has always been an integral part of daily life here, as much for subsistence as sport. Bitterns once provided the Sunday joint for workers but were hunted to extinction in the 1880s; and coot, its skin rich in the proteins so badly needed by an undernourished population living on the bread line, were shot to be made into a stew that was almost a staple. It is only in the past few decades, as we have increasingly taken on the environmentalist mantle, that hunting has fallen from favour. As a boy, Prince Charles and Prince Philip were regulars at the winter coot shoots organised at Whiteslea, a beautiful thatched lodge near the entrance of the broad. So, too, was Peter Scott. Yet despite a centuries-old tradition of slaughter, Hickling has played in the modern "green" movement a role so globally important that it can never be overstated. The paradox is easily explained: Good shooting, as Brendan Quayle observed in his book Wetlands, requires good conservation. And the whole notion of conservation owes its genesis to the vision of three peers and their remarkable gamekeeper.

The peers in question were milords Grey (Foreign Secretary and founding father of the League of Nations), Montagu (architect of Indian independence) and Lucas. In the early years of the 20th century, this triumvirate of naturalists and wildlife writers bought Whiteslea and 1,300 acres of Hickling Broad and its surroundings. Yes, it was a shooting estate; but it was also a private nature reserve, one of the first in the world and one that became a prototype for reserves everywhere. These far-seeing men were given even greater vision by the presence of a marshman called Jim Vincent, who was employed to manage both the shooting and conservation on the estate. Vincent helped create a magical place that brought the great and the good of the kingdom to Hickling; indeed, Peter Scott was so influenced by Whiteslea that it led him to help found the World Wildlife Fund and his own Wildfowl Trust. The bag at Vincent's shoots was extraordinary - 1,000 birds, including swans, was not uncommon, the haul being distributed among the villagers. The wonderful habitat of healthy reedbeds and marshes, well-managed carr and unpolluted broad - the largest sheet of open water in the region - meant that despite the killing, bird numbers remained buoyant.

Vincent epitomised the classic Broadlander. Not only was he an expert shot, he was no mean naturalist. He kept a passionately-observed wildlife diary for more than 30 years in which he recorded 247 species of bird. The journal was later published with paintings by the eminent Royal Academician GE Lodge.

Hickling was also the place where the great amateur naturalist Emma Louise Turner did much of her pioneering work as a wildlife photographer and it was she who, in 1911, found the first bittern's nest to be seen in Hickling's reed-rond since the bird's Victorian extermination. Needless to say, Vincent, who had found one the same year at nearby Sutton Broad, was one of her helpers.

Whiteslea and its estate was bought in 1944 by the millionaire philanthropist Christopher Cadbury, who gave it to the Norfolk Naturalists' (now Wildlife) Trust the following year. He later acquired Martham Broad for the trust, one of more than thirty conservation sites in Britain that he bought for the nation. Cadbury died in 1995; his family still lease the lodge from the NWT.

This astonishing legacy - aided and abetted by the navigational obstacle of Potter Heigham bridge - has meant that the ecology of Hickling and its upper Thurne neighbours remains closer to its former purity than other more accessible stretches of water. Hickling is also one of the few locations in Broadland where the marshman's craft is still practised. David Jenkin is one of the new generation who are proud of learning "the old ways" but who insist they do so within a modern perspective, although for outsiders like me it can seem like walking into a time-warp as the talk turns to meags, cromes, dydles and hodders - which turn out to be nothing more arcane than jargon for reed-cutters' tools.

David is the son of a serviceman and grew up at RAF Coltishall just a few miles from here on the Bure. He landed the job at Hickling after joining a Youth Training Scheme when he left school. Standing on the edge of a reedbed that his colleagues Gerald (who has since died) and Steve were harvesting, David, his face ruddied by windburn and cold, surveyed the golden stems from eyes

almost invisible in the shadow of a thick woollen hat and said: "I love this place. When I first came here I couldn't believe how big it was - humongous. But I took to it like a duck to water. It's a great life, cutting reed and sedge, clearing tree stumps, maintaining the reserve, all the conservation work. And I get paid for doing it."

When I was young, history and tradition were subjects for contempt. For David, however, they are to be treated with respect. "I'm aware of continuing the old ways of the marshmen," he said, "but we mostly rely on modern methods now, using tractors and cutting the reeds by machine, although Gerald always preferred to cut by hand - he has for more than twenty years. It's backbreaking work but I'd be sad to see the old ways die out. The cut reeds still have to be tied by hand. Steve can do a shoove (a bundle that measures two feet round the base) every three minutes and that includes stripping out all the debris and dead stuff from each one. We cut reed in January, February and March. It can get incredibly cold - I've been out here when it's been minus 14 - but February is often a write-off because you can't cut when the reed's too wet. Then we have to stop in March because the new shoots start to come through and we could damage them, which would affect next year's crop. We usually get about 10,000 shooves, although this winter we only had about 5,000 because last year was so dry."

Most of the reeds are sold to a local thatcher at £1.85 a shoove; a few are sold for fencing. Once the cutting is over, David and his team flood the area and leave it until next year's harvest when it is drained again.

David, like Vincent before him, is an innate naturalist. As we spoke, his eyes moved ceaselessly around him, now following a bearded tit flitting among the frond, now catching sight of a reed bunting perched on a stalk bent almost double beneath its weight. And he spoke with infectious delight as he described how he had watched a pair of courting marsh harriers performing their astounding sky-dance the previous spring.

"I'm really lucky to have a job with a salary, even though it isn't very much," he said. "In the past, guys used to cut the reeds no matter how terrible the conditions were - they had to, they were on piecework. If they didn't cut, they didn't get paid."

But even in a more liberal age, the work remains gruelling - and sometimes downright dangerous. This was brought home to me when I offered David a cigarette as we watched the cutting. He looked shocked and said darkly: "We never smoke out here." This was unusual - a non-smoking outdoorsman. But he explained: "Reeds burn like the sugar-cane in that car ad on telly. I know of one bloke who was lucky to escape with his life after a reedbed caught fire. He ran flat out in front of the flames and only just made it to the gate. It was as fast as him, you see." I put the cigarette back in the packet bloody fast.

I left David, Gerald and Steve loading shooves on to a trailer and walked back along the reed-fringed boardwalk to the reserve's visitor centre, pausing whenever the rond opened up to offer gorgeous views across the sunlit broad. The water was preternaturally calm on this March day; it was back to its more usual self when I crossed it by motorboat a few days later, the waves, whipped up by a fiendish nor'easter, beating against the windshield.

The reserve is run by the NWT's resident warden, John Blackburn, who, when I first met him, had arrived at Hickling only a few weeks earlier after spending eight years doing conservation work in heathlands of West Norfolk. He was filled with enthusiasm for his new home. "It's a marvellous spot," he said, "and we have a great team here. The reserve is open every day, so it's hard work; but it's also incredibly rewarding."

He is under no illusions about the work that needs to be done to keep the reserve ecologically healthy. One of its more immediate problems - quite apart from the general hazards of eutrophication and pollution - is ochre. Anyone who has paid a visit in recent years to Hickling or, more dramatically, to Horsey cannot but have been appalled by stretches of bright orange water. This, say many scientists, is caused by drainage ditches being dug too deep and is, in effect, rust. The NWT at Hickling is pioneering a form of treatment so simple that it seems too good to be true: sacks are stuffed with pine-bark chips, put into wire cages and sunk in dykes to act as giant blotters to trap the oxidisation. "It's very much at the experimental stage," John said. "The ochred water is not a pretty sight and although weeds seem to flourish in it, we do need to clean it up. We are hopeful these sacks could be the answer. There is no doubt that the water quality is improving but there is still a lot to do."

"A lot to do" applies across the board at Whiteslea. Scrub has threatened to engulf the fens and we watched teams of volunteers hacking down sallow and hurling the discarded wood on to a huge bonfire. Konik ponies, transferred from the Bure marshes, graze in the marshes clearing woody shrubs. There is an important caveat to this policy, however, one shared by wardens throughout Broadland: "We must not start gardening. We have to keep it natural."

The success of such a policy comes only at a price. The reserve sells reeds to raise capital, receives a modest return from entrance fees and local contributions and has applied for a grant from National Lottery funds (which it later received). John said: "A grant would make a huge difference. For instance, a roundabout can cost £800,000; we could do incredible things with that kind of money in terms of clearance, maintenance, restoration."

But dealings with Government-backed organisations require American-style administration: management plans, mission statements and hour-by-hour manpower projections, not to mention bewildering accountancy programmes. John smiled wrily. "You have to work within the bureaucratic framework if you want grants - and we do want grants. Even a wooden rowing boat costs thousands these days."

The answer revealed an inherent talent for diplomacy, an invaluable skill in an area of so many vested interests. Consider, for example, the case of windsurfers. Although not overburdened with large boats, Hickling Broad, with its relatively clean water and its exposure to North Sea winds, is often chockablock with sailboards which, to a canoeist like me, can be a real hazard. With all the polish of a practised public relations executive, John said: "They can be a problem because, like anglers, they get into the smaller bays where most boats don't venture and they put up the wildfowl, which is particularly bad news in the breeding season. We talk to them and hopefully we get through to them. But you can't please all of the people all of the time."

Most of the people who visit the reserve seem to be birders; its bitterns, beardies, reed buntings and occasional ruffs are justly renowned. But Whiteslea is also home to the rare swallowtail butterfly, a myriad species of unusual wetland insects and a number of almost extinct marsh plants, all of which attract specialist observers. John is anxious to make sure these latter feel as much at home at Whiteslea as the birders. He said: "We are working to restore a balance between the needs of everyone who comes here."

This may seem to be a dream job for a nature enthusiast but there is a down side: John is expected to be omniscient. He recalled the first time he took a group of visitors out on to the broad in a reed-lighter, one of Whiteslea's most popular attractions. "I was asked an impossibly detailed question about something I knew nothing about. I suppose I could have tried to bluff it out but I decided it was best to put up my hands and ask if any of the other passengers knew the answer. Someone did, of course. I've had the same experience since."

Once upon a time, an estate the size of Whiteslea would have provided work for dozens of men; but John does not share the bogus nostalgia for that bygone age. He said: "When this place was privately owned there used to be a lot of forelock-tugging and most people really lived hand-to-mouth in the harshest conditions. I'm glad those days are gone."

After saying our farewells, John went back to work with a tractor loaned to the reserve by its nearest neighbour, Willow Farm. It was here that I stayed when I first came to the Broads in 1967. The present owner, John Tallowin, was at agricultural college at the time of that visit but he has lived and worked on the farm all his life, taking it over when his father died in 1981. All but a hundred of his 420 acres are given over to beet, potatoes, peas, wheat and winter barley. The remainder is mainly marsh, woods and rough grazing.

The Broads Authority pioneered (that word again) a programme by which farmers were paid not to plough up grazing marshes, a scheme that led to the creation of Environmentally Sensitive Areas which are now found in regions containing endangered habitats throughout Britain. John is a keen advocate of the ESAs and is quick to emphasise his "green" credentials - a phrase he would never, I suspect, use himself. He is also a passionate advocate against the widely-held view that environmental damage is largely the work of farmers.

As we sat in his cosy kitchen drinking tea and eating Marmite on toast, he said: "Farmers should not be condemned for the poor water quality in the Broads. People say it is because we put too many nitrate-based fertilisers on the land which then drain off into the water. I admit that may be part of the problem; but the real offenders are phosphates that come from household detergents and soaps. People ask why farmers don't use organic methods but many organic fertilisers are very heavy in nitrogen. Until the 40s and 50s all farming was organic; but the Government brought in chemicals because they needed to feed the nation."

Farmers face a strange dilemma, compliments of Brussels and Westminster. On the one hand the European Union's Common Agricultural Policy gives them incentives - that is to say, cash - to reclaim land to produce pretty but largely worthless crops such as rape; on the other, they are rewarded for restoring grazing marsh. Such policies seem a clear contradiction. But John insists that the pursuit of profits has not had an adverse effect on the environment. "We do our bit," he said. "We don't grow things like rape and yes, we have taken out some hedges to make fields bigger. But we have also planted many others, which we keep trimmed and tidy. I think the character of this place has hardly changed over the years."

What has changed is its efficiency. During the 1960s and 1970s, grants from the Ministry of Agriculture, Fisheries and Food allowed John's father to underdrain the farm so that it can retain moisture throughout the summer - a crucial development in what is the driest county in England. But did this draining lead to the blight of ochre? "I don't think so," John replied. "There was a problem with it before the draining, so perhaps it's natural."

John also dismissed the popular myth of farmers' parsimony. He said: "Our drainage rates alone are £4,000 a year and it's hard work running this farm with only one other worker. But that's what you have to do if you want the lifestyle." He boosts his income with two holiday cottages that he leases out and two sheds of broiler chickens. Plans for another pair of sheds were vetoed by the Broads Authority following a few local protests. The veto highlights another agricultural dichotomy, best expressed by John's wife Viv when she said: "People want our produce but they don't want their view spoiled."

The view from Willow Farm remains unspoiled. A small mill stands at the edge of the broad where John's brother Roger and I used to camp in the summer. It was once the studio of the noted Broadland artist Rowland Green and still bears his name. But John and Viv get little chance to enjoy the scenery. He said: "We could sit here and look out at the water and watch the swallowtails flying past but we hardly ever have the time. When I was a boy I was always out fishing or boating or shooting. We go out sailing occasionally but really we don't get much chance."

His mother still lives in the village, which is a picturesque collection of cottages with two pubs, shops, a church, a large mill and the remains of a 12th century priory. But Hickling-born residents are becoming scarce as outsiders move in and push up house prices. John said: "The sad thing is that the old village structure has gone. When I was a child, every boy had a gun and used to come and shoot on Hickling Wall. Now you don't see that because the village is full of retired people and newcomers. But who knows - perhaps it's a good thing. Live and let live, that's what I say."

John is, at heart, an optimist. He said: "The water quality in the 70s had declined very badly but it is getting better slowly. There is still a long way to go. The reeds round the broad are still dying back and that is not just because of chemicals - cruisers play a part, too. But the Broads Authority can never put things back the way they were earlier this century. And anyway, no one wants to go back."

Since I spoke to David and the two Johns, something extraordinary has happened at Hickling. The investment made in cleaning up the water appears to have been repaid with spectacular interest, for the broad and its surrounding waterways have become clogged with varieties of rare stonewort and holly-leafed naiad to such an extent that only the smallest of boats can make any headway at all. No one is quite certain how this floral inundation happened, although some experts believe the plant's minute seeds may simply have lain dormant for years in the mud, in the same way that the seeds of desert flowers can lie in the sand for generations before sprouting.

The eruption has been greeted with joy by conservationists; but it has been greeted with consternation by the boating lobby, who insist that the "weed" is cut back sufficiently to allow proper marine access. The problem for them, however, is that the plants are subject to protection by European legislation to which local laws must defer; therefore, no order can be made to clear even a channel until there has been some kind of legal review - which could take years.

In the meantime, fleet-owners fear the continuing improvements in water quality throughout Broadland could mean that the plants spread swiftly down the Thurne and choke up other, more popular, stretches of water, in direct contravention of the lawful navigation rights that are one of the basic tenets of Broadland's national park status.

The issue remains unresolved at the time of writing; but I cannot help feeling that it sums up the dilemma of Broadland's administrators inasmuch as what should be a cause of celebration may, in fact, turn out to be a cause of much consternation and embarrassment.

seven

The Bure from Thurnemouth to Great Yarmouth is not, to put it mildly, everyone's cup of tea, flowing between vast marshes beneath huge skies. If you do not care for flatness, this is not the place for you. Even Arthur Ransome, that most dedicated of Broads' lovers, dismissed it in his Coot Club books as "the dreary lower reaches of the Bure".

It is not without its charms, however. Acle, which has the only road crossing between Wroxham and Yarmouth, is a bustling little town. A bridge has stood here since 1101 - criminals were once hanged from it and their spirits are said still to haunt the river - and the town's furniture market has its roots in the 13th century. It is also the scene of a pioneering sewage works, in which reedbeds are used as natural filters for processing waste.

Downstream is Stokesby, which is built around a green the size of a football pitch lined on three sides by pleasant brick houses and on the fourth by the river.

Between the towns, on the left, is Muck Fleet, an aptly-named stagnant dyke, now dammed off, linking the Bure to the Trinity Broads of Ormesby, Rollesby and Filby.

Ormesby was the setting of one of the biggest biomanipulation experiments carried out in the national park. For two winters in the mid-1980s, ten tons of fish were removed from the broad so that their natural prey, the water flea, could feed unmolested on algae that have clouded so much of Broadland's nutrient-enriched water. By the following spring, the broad was noticeably clearer.

Rollesby has traces of occupation dating back 4,000 years. It also has an 18th century workhouse, built "For the Instruction of Youth, the Encouragement of Industry, the Relief of Want, the Support of Old Age, and the Comfort of Infirmity". Such euphemistic twaddle could have been reduced to three words: House of Pain.

Filby is host to two of the area's biggest tourist draws. Thrigby Hall, a Victorianised mansion that looks more like a municipal office than a home, has a collection of some of the world's rarest animals, including Sumatran tigers and snow leopards. The hall was

once owned by a senior Royal Navy officer, Richard Sawbridge, who achieved notoriety in 1935 when he was court-martialed after his ship, Renown, collided with another in the Mediterranean. But the court decision was soon reversed and Sawbridge was promoted to Rear Admiral. Nearby is the Bygone Village, a supposed recreation of a village of Olde England but in reality a manifestation of the trend towards turning our countryside into a heritage theme park. Suffice to say, it is not one of my favourite places, for it seems to me to symbolise the phoney nostalgia that infests too much of Broadland and prevents the region finding a realistic identity as it faces the appalling problems it must overcome if it is to have a future.

Stracey Arms Mill is a restored four-storey tower, built on 40ft piles in the marshy ground, and houses an exhibition about the mills of Norfolk. It also offers spectacular views across the flatlands. Looking north-east, one can see the tower of Caister Castle, home of Sir John Falstaff, who declares, in the poet Robert Nye's eponymous and wondrously funny novel: "I love this Caister country. Miles and miles and miles of bugger all." The castle, which has a splendid car collection, was taken over after Falstaff's death by the Pastons, whose letters detailing daily life in the Middle Ages provide a unique archive for social historians.

To the right are Halvergate Marshes, the scene of one of the great environmental confrontations in the history of the national park. The marshes are best seen on foot, for the Weaver's Way, a long-distance footpath that dissects Broadland, passes across them from Yarmouth to Acle. These have been grazing marshes for centuries. Daniel Defoe, creator of Robinson Crusoe, visited the area in the early 18th century and was amazed by the number and size of Scottish cattle that were rested here on their way to Smithfield market in London. He wrote in A Tour Through England And Wales: "They... grow monstrously fat and the beef is so delicious to taste that the inhabitants prefer them to English cattle." But the marshes were threatened in the 1980s when local farmers were encouraged, with grants from the Common Agricultural Policy, to drain the land and grow crops. Eco-warriors joined forces with bureaucrats to fight the move - and eventually Westminster changed the rules and gave the Broads Authority the right of veto over drainage schemes.

The battle highlighted the mind-boggling array of red tape that exists in the region, particularly where its chief resource, water, is concerned. Decisions on its use sometimes need to be ratified by landowners, estate managers, parish, district and county councils, the local internal drainage board, the water board, the Environment Agency and the Broads Authority - and, if they cannot agree, by Whitehall and/or the EU. It's a miracle anything at all is achieved.

The Battle for Halvergate threw up two "heroes" from apparently opposite sides of the spectrum: Professor Aitken Clark, chief executive of the Broads Authority, and Andrew Lees, a Friends of the Earth activist. Prof Clark, nothing is not a diplomat, was credited with his behind-the-scenes negotiations that persuaded Westminster to change the rules; Lees, a Broadlander who had already cut his eco-teeth when he exposed a company in Norwich for dumping toxic waste in the Yare, led the peaceful direct action of the environmental demonstrators at Halvergate, producing irrefragable scientific evidence to back their case and masterminding the hugely successful media campaign.

The marshes were saved - and epitomise the spirit of optimism that still prevails, for the battle proved that despite the bureaucratic minefield of water management, all sides can work. In the aftermath, the Broads Authority introduced a scheme by which they paid farmers and land-managers £50 an acre for grazing marsh. The scheme later evolved into the nationwide Environmentally Sensitive Area programme.

There is, however, a sad end to the story: Lees, whose passion for conservation took him on perilous expeditions around the world, died of a suspected heart attack aged 45 in 1994 while investigating mining damage to the threatened forests of Madagascar.

Halvergate marshes lie between the Bure and the Yare. These reaches of the Bure have some wonderfully evocative names that sum up its wildness: Scare Gap and No Man's Friend, for example. It also has one called Slut's Haven, which may hark back to the days of hard-living wherrymen. The marshes reach the Yare at Berney Arms, a pub that stands next to a 70ft black-painted brick mill - the tallest windpump in working order in the UK - and the country's smallest railway station. The station is a monument to Victorian entrepreneurial duplicity. A farmer, by name Berney, sold land to the rail company on condition a station was built there. The firm agreed but, having received his signature, told him trains would not stop there. Berney pursued his case through the courts for a decade and finally, in 1855, a compromise was reached - the trains would stop by request only. The rule still applies.

The line is used primarily by walkers heading for the Weaver's Way and by birdwatchers bound for the Royal Society for the Protection of Birds' reserve which lies along the Yare where it opens out into Breydon Water, a huge estuarine mudflat that also receives the Bure and the Waveney before issuing into the North Sea at Yarmouth. The water always looks jet black and the tides are exceedingly fast, with a vertiginous rise and fall; not a day goes by without seeing at least one unhappy boat "on the putty", the local dialect for becoming stranded on Breydon mud. I have never had either the courage or the stupidity to canoe the estuary, although the great amateur naturalist Arthur Patterson regularly plied these treacherous waters in a small boat. Patterson, using the absurdly self-deprecatory pseudonym John Knowlittle, wrote what are considered the seminal wildlife books Through Broadland In A Breydon Punt (1920) and Wildfowlers And Poachers. In fact, he was one of a line of amateurs stretching back to the early 19th century when two well-to-do brothers, CJ and James Paget, the latter an eminent surgeon, wrote A Natural History of Yarmouth. It was a ground-breaking tome, listing alphabetically every living species they found within a 10-mile radius of their home town.

Breydon - indeed all the Yare marshes - is world famous for its birdlife. Ten of thousands of ducks, swans, geese and waders winter here and many hundreds more breed on the marshes. It is particularly noted for its very rare Bewick's swans. Numbers had been plummeting before the RSPB set up its Berney reserve in 1985. A count that year revealed there were only 41 left. But two years later, the population had soared to 700. Take it from me, as a canoeist who has been on the receiving end of angry swan, albeit a mute, that is a heck of a lot of bird.

The RSPB now manages a great deal of the marshland that flanks the north bank of the Yare between Yarmouth and Norwich and, in common with all Broadland's land managers, finds itself increasingly reliant upon public relations. The trouble is that with so many organisations involved in the day-to-day running of the Broads, everyone has their own idea of what is best, which often provokes opposition from other groups. Bank-raising is a prime example. The RSPB is generally in favour of this because it prevents polluted water upsetting the delicate ecology of reserves that support, say, bitterns. But other managers point out that raising banks would raise water levels in the Yare and flood their land. So what is the solution?

Chris Durdin, a regional official of the RSPB based at the charity's Norwich office, is keenly aware of the problem. "Some of our policies have caused controversy," he admitted, "but conservation is about making value judgements. In the end, though, there is a general concensus that the Broads are at risk. The Broads Authority has brought together the vested interests and with Aitken Clark you have a supreme diplomat. It's been said that the chief executive of the authority has to have asbestos fingers and a stab-proof

A member of Mundesley Camera Club

back. But in ten years time when Aitken has gone, who knows what will happen?"

Chris was pleased that more and more farmers in Broadland's grazing marshes are embracing conservation and that larger grants are now available for traditional livestock farming and for environmentally-friendly actions such as reducing nitrate fertilisers. "But," he said, "whether all this is too late to save the Broads remains to be seen." The key, he believes, is to be open-minded and to take an overview. "The trouble is," he added, "too many people keep to their own areas. For example, ask a warden on the Bure the last time he came to the Yare."

The Yare is a wide and busy river, not as crowded as the Bure but with enough traffic to keep a canoeist on his toes. It is also, especially in its lower reaches, hard graft for those relying on muscle power because the tides run rapidly and if you get your times wrong, a gentle outing turns into something reminiscent of the labour of Sysiphus.

The first port of call on the journey upstream is Reedham, opposite which is the New Cut, a two-and-a-half mile canalised link to the River Waveney dug in the 1840s. It was commissioned after Mutford Lock opened the Broads to sea traffic by way of Lowestoft, whose burghers, noticing that Breydon Water was silting up, saw the chance of stealing a march on their rivals in Great Yarmouth to serve the still-bustling port of Norwich. Their scheme was backed eagerly by the city fathers of the county capital, for it offered them a means of evading what they considered to be the outrageous shipping toll imposed at Yarmouth.

Unfortunately for both Lowestoft and Norwich, their intended dupes saw through the plot, Breydon was dredged, the dispute over taxes was resolved and the New Cut was a financial disaster. It has never really recovered; even today, it is in constant danger of silting up and closure unless millions of pounds are poured into its restoration.

Reedham was once a Roman seaport and was the traditional seat of the Anglo-Saxon king Edmund the Martyr who, like thousands of his countrymen, perished at the hands of the Vikings. Edmund was dispatched swiftly - unlike many of his subjects, for a favourite party trick of the Norsemen was to herd their unhappy victims into the local church, barricade the doors and torch the building. Nonetheless, Christianity prevailed and Reedham's parish church, St John the Baptist, manages to bridge the religious divide by incorporating into its 14th century walls many tiles said to come from a Roman pharos. The church once had lovely 16th century Dutch glass but it was wrecked in a fire as recently as 1981.

Pettits Animal Adventure Park is just north of the town while to the west lies Reedham's most famous asset: the only car ferry left on the Broads. It is owned by the Ferry Inn and is the only vehicular crossing between Great Yarmouth and Norwich.

When I passed by, the ferryman of more than 30 years, Mr Raymond Stone, was looking forward nervously to retirement. Mr Stone is a burly local boy, his shoulders as broad as his accent, who began his working life on the railways. Dr Beeching put paid to a promising career in the early 1960s and Mr

Stone found work in the paint shop of a firm making window frames. "Then out of the blue," he said, "I saw an advert for a ferry-man. I got the job and never looked back."

Three decades of plying the Yare in all weathers and at all hours have rendered Mr Stone what can only be called weather-beaten. His large face is lined and burned by wind, frost and sun; but his eyes sparkle and his mouth is permanently creased in a smile. He talks of his ferry, a chain-link 37-footer capable of carrying 12 tons, like a London cabbie: "You'll never guess who I had on the boat the other day..." His passenger list includes many minor celebrities who have done summer seasons in end-of-the-pier shows at Yarmouth - Charlie Drake, Russ Conway and Jess Conrad, to name but a few.

Mr Stone plainly enjoys a celebrity of his own. He has often been interviewed by journalists for newspapers, radio and television and the ferry has featured in a number of cinema films; which is some consolation for the harsh conditions in which he has had to work. "It gets very raw sometimes," he said with commendable understatement. "And when the wind is in the east in winter, it's not fit for man nor beast."

The Yare rarely freezes solid but its edges often ice over, making landing the ferry a problem. "I have to lay planking down when I can't get right up to the ramps," he said. "It's the same when the river floods." There were once greater hazards: large ships that commuted between the North Sea and Norwich. Nowadays the freighters have mostly gone and the biggest problems are caused by small boats, caught on a rapid tide, bumping

Raymond Stone

into the ferry, despite plenty of warning signs on the riverbanks both sides of the crossing. Other accidents happen, too. Mr Stone, his face taking on the quality of his name, recalled watching a little girl fall off a boat near the ferry as her mum was mooring. "The girl was struggling because she was wearing boots," he said, "so I threw her a lifebelt and shouted to her mother. But the woman was more worried about her boat than her child - I suppose she thought there were plenty more where her daughter came from. I was so angry I had to walk away or I'd have sworn at her."

Hardley Cross is as weatherbeaten as Mr Stone. It stands inside a small circle of railings at the entrance to the River Chet and marks the old borough boundary between Great Yarmouth and Norwich, whose mayors once used to meet here annually to settle watermen's disputes. The cross, which dates back to 1676, is also thought to mark the western end of Breydon before drainage reduced that vast expanse of water. The Chet is navigable for only three and a half miles to Loddon and Chedgrave - and that is only because it was dug out by navvies in the late 19th century so that wherries could reach the two towns. It is a sad irony that so much hard labour was employed on a white elephant, for within a handful of years the railways had wrecked the wherry trade.

Hardley Flood lies on the right bank midway up the Chet, a large piece of open water caused by flooding in the 1920s and now a waterbird wonderland. In just a few minutes, I saw shovellers, lesser black-backed gulls, teal, pochard and greylag geese furrowing the shallow waters while the reeds rang with the songs of warblers and buntings. A pair of sparrowhawks hunted in a copse nearby.

Loddon is a market town of Georgian houses, a splendid mill - now defunct - and a 15th century parish church, Holy Trinity, which contains a poor box made from a single piece of oak that is said to be the oldest in Britain. John Wesley, the founder of Methodism, preached in the town regularly. Much of it would still be familiar to him - with the exception of the square, which has been turned into a ghastly car park.

Chedgrave also has some fine old houses and a strange church, All Saints. Its squat tower is adorned with a thatched prism and its main body is a vivid cocktail of red brick and flint that looks charming but, in a new building, would attract the universal opprobrium of architectural purists today. Its windows contain 17th century glass from the magnificent French cathedral of Rouen.

This glass was the gift of Lady Beauchamp-Proctor, who lived nearby at Langley Hall and was one of the great landowners of the region. Langley has its own dyke, a tree-lined backwater that is a pleasant stopover for customers of the pretty Wherry Inn. Hardley dyke lies midway between the two. A footpath runs along the banks of the Yare from Hardley Cross to the dyke, although it is prone to becoming overgrown with nettles, teasel and treacle mustard; when I tried it one June morning, the string-like branches of the latter made it near-impassable and a walk of perhaps a mile took me rather more than an hour. But the struggle was worth it, for Hardley boasts a delightful small church, some fine Georgian houses and the most marvellous hedgerow I have seen - a kaleidoscope of red, gold, white, pink, mauve and green, compliments of, among others, an abundance of campions, poppies, and mallows. The effect was marred, however, by a pair of foul yellow-brick cottages.

These are nowhere near as foul, however, as the blot on the landscape on the other bank of the Yare: the British Sugar refinery at Cantley. Cantley's problem is not one of size, for it is smaller than many another; nor is it one of style, for it is no more unsightly than most industrial complexes; rather, it is one of geography, for it sits in the middle of a huge flatland and is a conspicuous, if not overwhelming, landmark for miles around. However, the plant is a vital provider of jobs so that what it lacks in cachet, it more than makes up for in cash. It is also the oldest refinery in Britain, extracting sugar from more than a million tons of beet a year.

Fleet Dyke, which leads to the private Buckenham and Hassingham Broads, is on the right past Cantley and the Beauchamp Arms marks where Buckenham Ferry used to operate until it was closed during the Second World War. The village's church, St Nicholas, once contained a 1290 bell, the oldest in Norfolk; it was stolen in 1973. Beyond the ferry, on the left, lies the first of two openings to Rockland Broad, one of only two publicly-accessible broads on the Yare. Cruisers are confined on Rockland to two narrow channels; canoes can explore the whole stretch, easing between the water lilies that are so thick in the middle that they look from a distance like an island. Rockland also has an alarming number of swans: my son Nicholas and I once counted forty. There is a private entrance from Rockland to Wheatfen, the site of a remarkable nature reserve and home of one of the most remarkable people in Broadland, indeed, anywhere: Phyllis Ellis, relict of perhaps the greatest of all the region's great amateur naturalists.

eight

No one, past or present, has had such an influence on the Broads as Dr Ted Ellis. The apogee of a constellation of amateurs who have been studying and cataloguing the wetland's wildlife since the early 19th century, Ted devoted his life to natural history. His living laboratory was Wheatfen, a 600-year-old ecosystem of primary Broadland that has never been put under the plough and that provides, almost uniquely, an insight into the area's pre-tourism ecology. His gift for imparting his passion for the Broads through his writing and broadcasting led to a new awareness of the region's fragility and is largely responsible for the "green" consciousness that is so much a part of Norfolk life today.

Ted's first love was mycology; and in the course of the forty years he lived at Wheatfen he collected 15,000 specimens of microfungi. Many were new to science and one species produced an antibiotic that works as an alternative to penicillin. He wrote a daily column for the Eastern Daily Press, never missing an edition, and was a regular contributor to The Guardian. He appeared regularly on television and radio, wrote innumerable articles for magazines and learned journals and was responsible for The Broads, the definitive study of the region.

Such a prodigious output would have filled two lifetimes for most folk; but not for Ted. He wrote much fine poetry, found time to raise seven children, entertained royally (including political exiles from around the world and a pantheon of leading naturalists such as David Bellamy and Sir Peter Scott), was a parish councillor, gave thousands of lectures and maintained a prolific global correspondence with experts and laymen alike. He also played host to a bizarre and ever-changing menagerie of injured birds and animals: visitors recall a one-legged heron in the hall, a wounded gull in the bath and a bittern in the engine house. His extensive library was home to a colony of pink spiders whose diet of book lice prompted Ted to describe them as "cherished guests".

So hectic a lifestyle can be a recipe for domestic chaos. But Ted, the visionary and poet, found his soulmate in his wife Phyllis.

A woman of astonishing energy and vitality, she was the perfect foil for her unworldly husband. She said: "Unlike Ted, I have absolutely no imagination. But give me a problem and I can usually work through it."

Such a talent allowed Ted the time and the lack of distractions to carry on the work that has had such an impact on official thinking in the Broads. Ellis died in 1986 in his 77th year - but his legacy did not die with him. Indeed, it was given new impetus by his widow through relentless promotion of his beliefs. From the time she gets up, usually at about 6am, until the time she goes to bed, often after midnight, she works tirelessly in the cause of conservation, writing letters, lobbying, lecturing, campaigning, organising and educating.

Yet such dedication to high ideals has not detached Phyllis from the human realm. She is charming, witty, erudite, fun-loving, intensely interested in other people and delightfully careless of material comforts. Her 18th century cottage had no mains water or electricity until the mid-1960s and the interior today is a helter-skelter of ancient furniture - "the sofa was second-hand when we bought it fifty years ago" - flowers, books, papers and pictures (including a wondrous embroidery, Sunset Over Breydon 1953, by Ted's mother Alice). But the house is undeniably a home. Where most people would have a television, a piano takes pride of place near an open fireplace adorned with hand-painted bricks. At various times, the cottage and its labyrinth of outbuildings has been home to Phyllis and Ted, their children, Ted's mother, Phyllis's father and a marshman called Russell who was born at Wheatfen and spent his last years there enjoying the legendary Ellis hospitality. Cosy contentment oozes from its walls.

Phyllis recalls with a smile: "The children were all terribly neglected as they grew up. They should have ended up in prison but they are all marvellous. We never had any money - I still don't - but we never went hungry. I am a genius at cooking cheap meals. In the days when coypu still roamed the Broads we sometimes had it casseroled with onions. It wasn't at all bad. And Ted had a dreadful coypu-fur hat. We could not afford a television but we made our own entertainment. We are all very musical. I play the piano, Ted sang with a silver baritone, just like my father, and the children played the banjo, guitar, flute and various kinds of Elizabethan woodwind. These were all played at Ted's funeral... it was a terrific do."

The house is surrounded by marsh, fen, carr and woodland and scientists from around the world flock to study this pristine wonderland. During one of my visits, confirmation came through from the Natural History Museum that a beetle found the previous year at Wheatfen was none other than galeruca interrupta, a species not seen in Britain for more than 80 years and officially listed as extinct.

David Bellamy once said: "Wheatfen is, in its own way, as important as Mount Everest or the giant redwood forests of North America." Phyllis shrugs off the tribute, claiming, with an ingenuous smile, that Bellamy was "exaggerating". But this is modesty - no one else seems in any doubt about the reserve's significance. Wheatfen is open all the time,

TED ELLIS
NATURE

which demands tremendous stamina from Phyllis and the reserve's warden, David Nobbs. But stamina is what Phyllis seems to have aplenty. I first met her a few days after I had slipped a disc and I could barely walk when I arrived. Phyllis, on the other hand, was a ball of fire, rowing me around the five miles of Wheatfen's waterways in her Norfolk punt, helping me crawl in and out of the boat and offering me her arm as we walked back to the house after our outing. At one stage, Phyllis, who is twice my age, slipped and fell but merely dusted herself down and carried on. I could not even bend to tie my laces without wanting to scream. It was a humbling experience.

Later, leaving me resting my back in front of the fire, she cooked dinner, answered innumerable phone calls, put the final touches to arrangements for one of the many day-visits by local schoolchildren, fixed a date to speak at a public inquiry into Broads Authority proposals to raise the river banks - "it's a disgrace, it will flood Wheatfen" - then dashed off to a parish council meeting to argue about the disputed ownership of a footpath. Phyllis returned just before 11pm, muttering dark imprecations against her opponents on the council. By this time, I was beginning to nod off; but Phyllis was just getting into her stride...

She said: "I don't sleep well. I used to write all my letters at three in the morning but now I just read cheap detective novels. It's the only chance I get to relax with a book because I am so busy. I have been doing about 30 talks a year, basing them on Ted's 20,000 slides, but I'm starting to scale it down because at my age you don't want to go out so much at night."

Wheatfen has, like everywhere else in Broadland, been affected by poor water quality caused by pollution and increasing salination. It lost its entire fish stock and otter population after the sea flooded the Broads in 1953, the water reaching the back door of the cottage. The fish later returned - the otters did not, although there was an unconfirmed sighting of one at Wheatfen in August 1997. It has also been damaged by what Phyllis angrily called the madness of legal mercury-dumping in the Yare in the 1960s and by the continuing problem of nutrient enrichment caused by fertilisers and household waste.

Furthermore, she says, "bureaucracy has gone mad - it's ridiculous how much paper is produced and wasted just on the parish council, for example. So yes, I get depressed sometimes. But in the end, I do believe people do their best and I believe that education is terribly important. I was a teacher for years at the local primary school and there is no doubt that children can be taught to be aware. I think that is where the best hope lies for the Broads."

The dykes that drain the fens look like something out of The African Queen. Reeds as tall as bungalows overhang the water and in summer the air becomes tropically hot. Mosquitoes live there in numbers befitting a biblical plague and rising tides make some areas downright dangerous, even to experts. For example, Phyllis had not been out on one of the marshes for ten years since she and two scientists became lost there as the tide roared in. It took the party two frightening hours to wade to safety.

But despite the discomforts and perils, this is a magical place of unsullied beauty and tranquillity, bursting with wildlife. Chinese water deer haunt the marshes but are almost invisible in the riotous undergrowth; Cetti's warblers roost in the waterside trees, their calls so loud that a BBC sound engineer had to muffle his microphone when the needle went off the dial as he tried to record them; rare orchids grow in the carr; in fact, the species of flora and fauna, many of them great rarities, are so diverse that they have brought worldwide fame and an unparalleled reputation to Ted, to Wheatfen and to Phyllis.

The Broads Plan, the official policy document on which the future of the area depends, is dedicated to Ted; and Phyllis was guest of honour at the launch ceremony in the spring of 1997. Prof Aitken Clark told me: "Ted was the gentle Gandhi of the Broads. He combined expertise with frailty. We need more people like him."

I asked Phyllis, who had received an MBE from the Queen the previous year, if fame brought unwanted pressures. She laughed dismissively. "I'm not famous - I'm a nobody. Ted was famous. He was offered high honours but he refused them. I was pleased to get the MBE and I'm not afraid to swing it to get what I need. And I'm not afraid to pester people if necessary."

Phyllis has dedicated her life to her husband, to her children and to Wheatfen. To some, it may seem a life led within unacceptably narrow parameters; to Phyllis, it is a life blessed by fortune. "I have always tried to do my best," she said. "Sometimes you just have to shrug your shoulders and say, To hell with it. But I have been very lucky. I never want to leave this place because I love it so."

nine

Immediately opposite the Ted Ellis Trust lies Strumpshaw Fen. The river frontage is part of a 2,000-acre reserve run by the RSPB. This place will always have a special place in my heart, not simply because of its beautiful reedswamp, marshes, fens and woodland but because it is where, after thirty years of trying, I saw my first bittern. It happened quite unexpectedly, as the best treats do, on a cold but sunlit January afternoon. Nicholas and I strolled into the hide overlooking the only stretch of unfrozen water on the reserve and there, not 50ft away, stood this bird that has become the most ubiquitous symbol of the Broads. It took us several

Dr Martin George

moments to realise what it was, for even at such proximity its brown-streaked plumage made it almost invisible among the reeds. I was awestruck - then amused. Emma Louise Turner, whom we have already encountered at Hickling, was spot-on when she wrote: "He appeared very ludicrous; for with his big green legs and splayed feet, drooping wings and head held high in the air, he looked like a tall, gaunt old woman masquerading in bird's attire."

Bitterns are the in-thing in Broadland. The European Union is pumping a small fortune into schemes to revivify reedbeds, their natural habitat, and the RSPB has sometimes imported eels for the birds because, since damming off the river, their staple diet is no longer available in the dykes and fens. This may seem a distorted approach to conservation; but Mike Blackburn, the reserve's warden when I visited - he has since moved on - is unrepentant, for the damming sparked an explosion of wildlife of every other kind. Mike, once a pesticide scientist for Shell, had worked for the RSPB at Strumpshaw since 1974, when he began the heroic labour of single-handedly banking in the entire reserve, which then covered 300 acres. It took him six years - and he was immediately rewarded when a pair of marsh harriers nested there the following spring. With a smile that somehow managed to avoid being smug, he said: "It was no accident that the one thing followed the other."

Mike, tall and extremely forthright, was also rewarded with an assistant to help guard the nest from the vile curse of egg-collectors. More staff were allocated as the RSPB took control of the marshes at Buckenham and Cantley and, across the river, at Surlingham. The upshot has been greater bio-diversity, cleaner water and ever-increasing visitor numbers. But it has a downside, too: Mike found himself with less time to do the practical work of conservation - bulldozers and chainsaws seem particularly appealing to him - because he had to do more and more paperwork. It is a subject to which he returned often; but any complaints could not disguise his enthusiasm for the reserve that had been his home for so many years. He was especially enthusiastic about bio-diversity. "We are not just interested in birds," he said. "We want to improve everything. I particularly love the plants. We have a burgeoning population of marsh pea, for example - that's really rare these days."

But it is birds that draw most of the reserve's 20,000-odd visitors every year; and it is a heck of a show on offer. Apart from the wintering bitterns, enthusiasts can see bearded tits, summer ospreys, Cetti's warblers, peregrine falcons that fly in occasionally to feed on the 10,000 wigeons that winter here; even, from time to time, passing red kites that have been reintroduced into England.

These last, still alarmingly rare, are much prized by oological onanists. They are also at risk from irresponsible gunmen. Mike's face turned to the colour of a kite's feathers as he said: "A local man shot one recently along with a buzzard. He was bragging about it in the pub to his mates but no one could prove anything. The police are watching him now - I hope they get him because he's a real twat."

The reintroduction of the kite is one of many projects for the future. Black-tailed godwits breed at similar sites in Holland and ruffs, spoonbills and storks have all nested here in previous centuries, when the ecology was in better shape.

But Mike was optimistic. "You have to be," he said, "or you couldn't do this job. But much of the conservation work only touches the surface. There are still too many chemicals in the river and we only use Yare water after flooding when it is heavily diluted. But it is better than it was - there was a time when 60 per cent of it at low water was effluent from the sewage works. But there is still a long way to go."

Mike came to Strumpshaw soon after the RSPB began renting the fen from a local landowner. The two parties signed the lease on the dining table at a nearby cottage which has been home since the early 1960s to Dr Martin George, scientist, one-time regional officer of the Nature Conservancy Council (now English Nature) and author of a staggeringly comprehensive study of the area called The Land Use, Ecology And Conservation Of Broadland, which was published at his own expense.

Martin, tall, distinguished and retired (though not retiring), tipped off the RSPB about the site. He recalled: "I used to do a bit of scrub-bashing on the fen and would chivvy up the owner to clear it. He eventually got sick of me and asked me if I wanted to lease the land. I couldn't afford it at the time so I pointed it out to the RSPB."

He signed up with what was then called the Nature Conservancy in about 1960. "We were the first official conservationists and I think I was regarded as a bit of an eccentric," he recalled. "People did not really know what to make of us. Some even thought we were some kind of nudist group." He laughed with delight at the memory. But the organisation's role is deadly serious. "The decision in the 60s not to make the Broads a national park was followed by a total impasse," he said. "The disparate bodies involved in it did not get on harmoniously and the Government came under intense pressure from groups like us, the Council for the Protection of Rural England, the Broads Society and the Norfolk Naturalists Trust to really get stuck into conservation. The politicians finally asked us to carry out a survey of the area."

The Nature Conservancy produced, in 1965, a Report On Broadland. "It was a definitive document," Martin said, "and we identified many of the problems with which we are familiar today: the threat to fens, the need for speed limits, drainage risks and reedswamp regression, for example, although I'm sorry to say we didn't know much at the time about nutrient enrichment. We recommended the creation of a Broads consortium, which was duly formed. Unfortunately, the plan they commissioned reckoned the Broads could take a huge increase in boat traffic and the thing just collapsed - there was no cohesion at all and the whole area started to go wrong."

A Broads consultative committee was set up in the mid-1970s and eventually an umbrella authority was formed. This body, however, had no control over navigation and the result was a great deal of friction. "Eventually," Martin said, "it was realised that we

would have to have a one-off body and the present Broads Authority was established."

The biggest problem today, he believes, is the bureaucratic wrangling over water - a common complaint, as we have already seen, throughout Broadland. "I'd like to see the Broads Authority responsible for water," he said, "which is, after all, our main amenity. At the moment, so much of what the conservationists are doing is reliant upon other bodies taking action. Nutrients will be a problem until we persuade the water companies to instal the right equipment, like phosphate-strippers. And we are having major problems with droughts because the water companies gambled on a wet winter and didn't impose a hosepipe ban in the summer. Well, the gamble failed. Now the Government is demanding a huge increase in new houses in Norfolk but fail to realise that East Anglia is the driest part of the country. The moral of the story is to do a little strategic thinking: we have to start contingency planning now to take water from elsewhere further west. It's a tremendously complicated undertaking but we are going to need it in ten years. Short-termism is awful."

Increasing salination, which affects all forms of wildlife, not just fish stocks, is another problem that worries Martin. So, too, does global warning. Summers will be hotter but winters will remain chilly and frosty. Crops like maize will become commonplace; but maize could not be drilled in Norfolk in the autumn because it is susceptible to frost, so much arable land would lie fallow throughout the winter. Martin said: "This will cause massive nitrogen loss from the fields and it will end up in the rivers, causing further problems. What we need is to encourage a healthy growth of waterweeds because they will lock up surplus nitrogen and the system will then more or less come into line naturally."

He also wants a barrier built across the Yare to safeguard the rivers - not to mention the tens of thousands of people and their homes in the Yarmouth area. "But I have given up any hope of seeing that in my lifetime," he added sadly.

Paradoxically, though, his vision of the future is not one of despair. "I mainly go on the doom and gloom side because I've been at the sharp end for so many years," he said, "but really I'm very optimistic because of the incredible build-up in our awareness of the environment - we are all environmentalists now. It is even seeping into government thinking. Some years ago I asked an official from the Ministry of Agriculture, Fisheries and Food if we could be grant-aided for conservation in the way that farmers got help from the Common Agricultural Policy to make land arable. He said, 'Over my dead body - if you want funding, find it yourself.' Five years later we had the ESAs."

These changes seem a source of constant wonder to Martin. As I was preparing to leave, he told me: "The Broads and the way they are run are a fascinating example of human folly. It's monstrously exhilarating."

Strumpshaw is just a few minutes downstream from Brundall, a busy riverside village dominated by its boatyards. Brundall was once famous for its pleasure garden and its fine array of specimen trees, most of which were planted by Dr Michael Beverley between 1881 and 1911 when he used the picturesque estate as a private retreat. It was later acquired by the entrepreneur Frederick Cooper who, shortly after the end of the First World War, opened it to the public, building a riverside hotel, tearoom, yacht basin and tennis courts. In their heyday in the 1920s, Brundall Gardens attracted up to 60,000 visitors a year. Many arrived by steamboat from Norwich or Great Yarmouth while others travelled by train to the specially-built Brundall Gardens Halt. The station is still used; the gardens are not and the few parcels of the land that have escaped later development are, at the time of writing, virtually derelict.

Away from the riverside, Brundall has become almost a dormitory town for Norwich; and amid its quiet streets of unpretentious houses lives one of Broadlands' most famous daughters, Dr Joyce Lambert, PhD, MA, latterly Reader in Biology at Southampton University until she retired in 1979.

Joyce made her name as the first person to realise that the Broads were not, as had previously been assumed, a natural phenomenon. This important discovery was the result of an extensive geomorphological and ecological survey of Broadland made in close collaboration with Joe Jennings, a lecturer at Leicester University who later emigrated to become Reader in Geomorphology at the Australian National University.

Joyce, who moved to Norfolk with her Norwich-born parents when she was eight and now lives in the house her grandfather built, said: "When we started our survey after the last war we believed, like everyone else, that the broads were natural lakes. But while I was drilling bore-holes through the fenland peat, I kept noticing that the basins of many of the broads had vertical peat sides reaching down to a level peat floor some three to four metres below the surface of the water. These steep sides had previously been unsuspected - they were hidden by vegetation and sealed in by deep mud. Although a few broads appeared to have naturally sloping sides immediately against the upland, these sharp edges kept turning up. We couldn't understand it.

"The maps and aerial photographs used in the survey also showed curious features - for example, the outlines of many broads had narrow, parallel peninsulas projecting into the open water, sometimes with small, elongated islands directly in line with them. To our surprise, we found that their direction matched the pattern of strip-parcelling we found in some of the old tithe maps. Close-set boring established that these peninsulas and islands had steep sides of peat like the margins of the broads and shallowly-submerged ridges of peat were often found extending from their ends. It was all very puzzling."

Joyce's Eureka moment came late one evening in her study at Cambridge University, where she held a research fellowship at the time. "The penny," she said, "suddenly dropped - the Broads must be man-made. All the anomalies could be explained if they were once the sites of great peat pits which were subsequently flooded. The steep peat sides would be the former working faces; the peninsulas, islands and ridges would be the remains of old peat balks left between adjacent workings; and the sloping landward margins

Dr Joyce Lambert

seen in a few of the broads would represent places where all the peat had been removed right down to the sloping valley side."

The revelation provoked an outcry, with many experts and Broadlanders refusing to believe the findings - some older locals are still sceptical. But the evidence continued to mount. Clifford Smith, a lecturer in historical geography at Cambridge, unearthed old documents that showed peat-digging was widespread in the region in medieval times, particularly in the 13th and 14th centuries. And from records such as ancient account-rolls he was able to calculate that there had been a peat industry big enough to have created all the basins that make up the broads today.

"It was terribly exciting," Joyce said. "Joe and I started work in the late 40s but we didn't realise the man-made nature of the broads until 1952. It took another eight years to collate our findings and prepare the work for publication and our Research Memoir for the Royal Geographical Society didn't appear until 1960. By that time, Joe had left for Australia, I had gone to Southampton and both of us had started work on different projects. But, of course, I came back to my Norfolk roots when I retired."

Much of Joyce's fieldwork was done across the Yare from Brundall on Surlingham Broad. This has two dykes from the Yare, both of which lead into Bargate, the only significant piece of open water on the broad. Bargate is the graveyard of 13 wherries and, eerily, many of their bones can be seen at low water. The magic of Surlingham for me, however, is its labyrinthine backwaters that are accessible only to small boats. Nicholas and I nearly became lost in our canoe one summer afternoon when a brisk breeze whipped up the water so that we could no longer see the current, the only way of navigating out of a maze that would have graced any Cretan Minotaur's curriculum vitae. We had not had the foresight of Theseus to bring a ball of cotton to mark our ingress.

We finally escaped with the bottom of our boat scraping the bed; Rodney Patrick had less good fortune. Rodney once had the eel rights to Surlingham Broad, as well as to Hickling and all the tidal rivers of the broads. He and his son, wearing only trousers and T-shirts on a balmy evening, were caught by a sudden fog. "I'd forgotten to look if the tide was in or out," he said, "and as night fell, the temperatures began to drop. We were freezing. We tried cutting reeds and lighting them on the water to get a few moments of heat but we were still cold. Then I had a brainwave. I covered us with a blanket of reeds, like a thatched roof. We were as warm as toast. When daybreak came, we found we were only a few yards from the entrance."

Rodney, gaunt and grizzled, lives with his petite wife Pearl in Hethersett. He caught eels as a child, using a ball of red wool threaded with worms or a bale of hay wrapped round the guts of two rabbits which, left in the water for a couple of days, always snared half a dozen fish. But his early adult years were spent in forestry, many of them in Holland, before he met Pearl, who had been involved in eel-fishing with a friend since 1979. The couple started fishing together in 1986, spending much of the year living on a 28ft cruiser and catching vast

Pearl and Rodney Patrick

quantities of eels in nets and setts whose ancestry can be traced back more than 500 years. "It was a great way of life," he said.

The couple are eel-lovers and speak with undisguised pleasure and respect about these most elusive and mysterious of creatures who live in thrall to the phases of the moon, who seem to possess a chameleon-like ability to blend into their surroundings, who are thought to migrate for thousands of miles across the Atlantic to the Sargasso Sea to breed, who manage to colonise gravel pits by crossing land during morning mist or a late shower and who, as mature "silvers", can be as thick as a strong man's forearm. Pearl described eels as "curious and nosey"; and she should know, for she made the wondrously artful Dutch fyke nets that they often deployed to catch their cunning quarry, a 6.5metre cone-within-a-cone into which the fish are lured and trapped. Rodney said: "Between May and August, you get a massive run once a month. They are livelier two days before a full moon and they are biting each other as you pull them out. Silvers don't usually run when the weather is normal - but on a terrible, wet, windy, thundery night, when the moon is right, they will run by the thousand and they will get out of their gravel pits and slither across the ground into the rivers."

Immature eels are normally green. Adults turn black in dark dykes, sandy-brown in gravel pits and they are silver when they take to the sea en route to their breeding grounds. "But I'm not convinced that they all go to the Sargasso Sea," Rodney said. "We've caught elvers that were an inch long and almost transparent - they could not possibly have crossed the Atlantic. And experts once tried tagging eels off the Norfolk coast to track them to the Sargasso; but instead of going there, they swam off up the Humber. The truth is, no one really knows what eels do. It's amazing."

One thing that Rodney does know, however, is that pollution has decimated the eel population of the Broads and wrecked his living. "The so-called experts," he said bitterly, "blame overfishing for the huge fall in numbers but that's a load of crap. The pollution everywhere round here is horrible now, utterly crazy. The wildlife on the Broads in the early morning used to be fantastic but that's also been affected by pollution. The last decent year's fishing we had here was 1989 or 90. We kept going for three or four years after that but we were getting back £100 for every £300 we spent. We had up to 140 nets once but dozens and dozens were nicked. They cost £90 to make so to lose twenty-five is a disaster. And there are fifty illegal nets for every licensed one. You could only fish now as a hobby or to help with dole money. The situation is so depressing. There is no possible way of eel-fishing getting back to the way it was." Pearl added with a sigh: "It broke our hearts when we had to sell our cruiser."

Alone among the people I talked to in Broadland, they see no hope for the future of the area; indeed, they are keen to emigrate. Rodney said sadly: "We could just scrape a living here - just, maybe - but really there's nothing left for us in this country now. We want to go and live and work in the forests in Germany on the Dutch border. They respect their countryside - we take ours for granted."

It was with a heavy heart that I left them. But, I reflected later as I returned to Brundall to pick up my canoe, most people seem determined somehow to pull the iron from the fire before it is too late and surely that enthusiasm will save the day. It was hard to keep that positive thought in my mind, however, as I paddled past the outfall of the Whitlingham sewage works. Mercury had once been pumped into the Yare from here - incredibly, it was legal at the time - and deposits of this most lethal of elements still lie beneath the mud of the riverbed like some ecological timebomb too volatile to be defused. I know things have changed for the better immeasurably since those dark days but it was still impossible to repress a shudder as I passed.

Next door to the outfall, locked between the Yare and Norwich's southern by-pass, lies Whitlingham country park, a 600-acre oasis of green which became, in 1997, the site of a new broad in a 10-acre flooded gravel pit. A second broad, of 81 acres, is due to be opened by 2006. Thorpe St Andrew stands opposite. Now a suburb of the county town, this one-time village was the birthplace in 1782 of Norfolk's most renowned artist, John Sell Cotman, and was also the site of Britain's oldest lunatic asylum, St Andrew's Hospital, built between 1811 and 1814. One can only imagine the horrors of this establishment - Hammer Films, I suspect, painted an overly romantic portrait of such institutions. One final curiosity. Near here, in 1874, the Yarmouth express ploughed into a mail train on the one-track line. The express may have been chugging along at only 35mph but 23 passengers died and scores more were injured in the disaster, the greatest railway tragedy of the time. An inquiry into the crash recommended that henceforth drivers must give signalmen a token so that these latter would know if any other train was on the line; the token system soon became common pratice nationwide.

This is the head of navigation on the Yare for most boaters. The Wensum, which takes you into central Norwich, goes off to the right; the Tas leads off to the left. This latter is an intriguing stream. Nowadays it is only a few feet wide and a few inches deep, yet once it was capable of carrying a fully-laden Roman galley to the imperial regional capital of Venta Icenorum a couple of miles to the south. Venta is worth a visit, although little remains of the bustling metropolis that was once home to thousands of people who came here from all over the known world under the Pax Romana. The 40-acre site, which is today dominated by medieval St Edmund's church, was once encircled with 20ft stone walls, the relics of which can still be seen in places, and was built at the heart of what had been the kingdom of the Iceni. The fortified city was commissioned after the Iceni queen, Boudicca, rebelled against the empire and sacked Colchester and London. She poisoned herself after her army was wiped out in an ambush by the Roman general Seutonius in AD60.

The town reached its zenith in the third and fourth centuries AD and featured among its houses and villas two temples, a market, shops, a forum, a glassworks, administrative offices, baths, a quay and, possibly, an amphitheatre. The town was abandoned and soon fell into ruin after the legions were recalled to Rome at the beginning of the fifth century. In the millennium that followed, stones from the imperial walls and buildings were carried away for Saxon, Viking and Norman homes and Roman tiles were also used in the walls of St Edmund's.

Venta owed its pre-Roman pre-eminence to a sacred wooden henge, immemorially old, that stood a mile away at Arminghall. The centrepiece of this monument, coeval with and as mysterious as Stonehenge or Avebury in Wiltshire - to which it is linked by the prehistoric Icknield Way - was a ring of eight yard-high logs, painted totemically and joined by lintels, that described a circle 50ft wide. It may even have been roofed. The whole was enclosed by two ditches eight feet deep with a maximum diameter of 120ft. The wood has long since rotted but modern scientific methods have enabled archaeologists to reconstruct an image of what must have been one of the wonders of Ancient Britain.

Mike Barnes and crew

ten

Venta's mortal remains are rather feeble when compared to those of its Roman sister at Burgh Castle, a third century AD fortress built on a rare piece of high ground in the reedswamp that carpets the land where the River Waveney, the final river of Broadland, flows out into Breydon Water.

Burgh Castle was one of the forts on the so-called Saxon Shore. Three sides of its huge walls are preserved almost intact, enclosing an area of some 200,000 square feet. Like Venta, it played host to people from across the world; among its last occupants before the imperial legions were withdrawn was a Yugoslav cavalry detachment, Equites Stablesiani. A little over two centuries after it was abandoned, an Irish missionary named Fursey built a small monastery within its walls in about 640 and spent ten years there before crossing the Channel to Gaul, where he died. According to the Venerable Bede, the most reliable of the early English ecclesiastical historians, Fursey was famous for his visions and foresaw that the earth would be consumed by the fires of falsehood, covetousness, discord and justice. One could uncharitably suggest that such pronouncements of the bleeding obvious are worthy of no one but a mountebank; but his dreams were the direct inspiration for one of the most sublime works of literature ever penned: Dante's Inferno.

The monastery was razed by a Viking contingent in 869 and a Norman motte and bailey was later built on the site. Later still, the place became known for its brickfields and cement works, which survived until the end of the 19th century.

The fort enjoys a matchless view across Haddiscoe marshes. The rond is about 100 yards deep and glows like a sea of gold in the sunshine. Berney Arms mill shimmers in the distance beside the quicksilver snake that is the Yare and the perfect flatness of the marshes highlights the multifarious silhouettes of mills and church towers. It also, sadly, underscores the monstrosity that is Cantley.

The Waveney marks the county border. Burgh Castle and everywhere else on the same bank is in Suffolk, while Haddiscoe and its compatriots are in Norfolk. It is, without doubt, my favourite Broadland river, largely because it is so underused. Canoeing here is idyllic, although the tides run fast and high the closer you are to Breydon. For those who prefer to remain on terra firma, the Angles Way runs the length of its valley from Yarmouth offering unspoilt views the whole way apart from its unpromising start on Cobholm Island, a gehenna of rundown allotments that is due to be what bureaucrats call "visually enhanced" - prettified, to you and me.

Fritton Decoy is on the left. It is a long, narrow lake, cut off from the river, that was originally a wildfowling centre but is now part of a country park run by the Somerleyton estate (of which more later). Fritton is famous for its cuckoos.

Further on, you reach St Olave's, the only riverside settlement of any substance fronting the Waveney between Yarmouth and Beccles. The village, named after an 11th century Danish king, is home to a tiny wooden trestle mill and the remains of an Augustinian priory, founded in 1216. This cenobitic community was never large; there were only five canon fathers there at the Dissolution. But it boasts an important and intact refectory undercroft that is a masterpiece of early English brickwork. Its vaulted ceiling is supported by columns of Purbeck marble, one of which rests on a Roman millstone.

The priory is reached up a grassy lane and stands beside an enclosure inhabited by South American ruminants; I think they were alpacas but they could just as easily have been llamas or guanacos. The same lane runs behind a handful of old wooden bungalows, one of whose ancestors was the summer childhood home of Phyllis Ellis, the chatelaine of Wheatfen, who used to swim the river every day before school. It would be a brave - and foolhardy - person who swam the river today.

The Waveney is traversed by a fine old iron bridge standing beside the boatyards that remain the lifeblood of the village. Mike Barnes, who now runs Southgate's yard at Horning, began his career as a boatbuilder here. Mike's love of Broadland started as a child on nearby Oulton Broad, which he explored in a perilously decrepit rowing boat propelled with one broken oar and a shovel - until it sank. After leaving school, Mike spent many years as a diver in the oilfields of the North Sea, an occupation that, in his own words, was "breathtakingly dangerous".

Realising that the longer he carried on diving the shorter the odds against an accident became, Mike resolved to retire from such death-defying gambling. But he did not give up gambling altogether and in a sentiment borne very much of the heart and not of the mind, bought on a whim the beautiful 1904 yacht Nathalie, which he still races today.

A last foray into the oil business resulted in a one-year pay-off that enabled him to clear his debts and taxes and enabled him, too, to employ a boatbuilder to restore Nathalie and to teach him the rudiments of his trade. Finally, in 1987, Mike and a friend bought the Albatross aluminium speedboat yard in St Olave's. They started by restoring old vessels but later began to build their own modern interpretations of 1930s Broads' yachts. Today, Mike and fellow enthusiast Phillip Davies run the Norfolk Broads Yachting Co from Southgates with a hire fleet of nearly three dozen boats, about half of which are restored classics.

He said: "The heritage business has been a revolution for us. There has been a resurgence of interest in the Broads and our traditional yachts are very popular. We have modern Tupperware boats, too, because they act as nursery boats for new holidaymakers who then often migrate to the older vessels. One of our most popular is Zoe; she was built in 1896 and is the oldest yacht left in hire on the Broads."

The company also runs the 1915 White Moth, the last wherry yacht to be built in Broadland. "I first saw her on Surlingham Broad in 1980," he recalled. "She was in a terrible state and needed a huge amount of work and money. Then I saw her again in about 1986 at St Olave's, by which time she was just a hulk. Maynard Watson rebuilt her in Horning over a period of about five years. She now continues to work in much the same way she did eighty odd years ago, although the local authority help us with some grant aid which basically covers insurance and the river tolls. It's rare to get a full week let of the wherry but we do a lot of weekends and short breaks."

He feels strongly about phoney nostalgia, saying dismissively: "You can't just recreate the past." But equally he believes that many aspects of Broadland life have changed little. "Our main customers are still people who first came here thirty or more years ago," he said. "There are some yobs - to some extent they have been here all along - but underneath, you still have the genuine holidaymakers whose general good nature hasn't changed in a hundred years. I suppose the real difference today is that people are much more ecologically aware. Non-greens are social pariahs, which they certainly weren't thirty years ago."

I asked him how much of Broadland can be returned to the pollution-free zone it once was. "From what time?" he replied. "After all, typhus was once common here and we don't want that back. The truth is, pollution is not so much to do with effluent as with intensive farming. And we are seeing increasing salination because river flows have fallen thanks to greater water abstraction, which is having a profound effect in some areas."

Cash, of course, is at the root of the problem. "Take the ESAs," he said. "ESA land is worth less than other farmland because the use of the land is limited, especially in the use of artificial fertiliser. Everyone wants to preserve the Broads but money has to support these ideals. If the farmer can't compete because his yield is lower without fertiliser or because he is only allowed to graze cattle for which there is no demand, then he should be compensated. I don't want to see anyone go out of business."

Red tape and American-style legal mania are also problems. The European Union's Recreational Craft Directive demands standardisation and is the marine equivalent of the loony Brussels ruling about bent bananas. "It takes away all individuality," Mike said. "And there is a worrying trend towards

litigation in all walks of life that could cause major difficulties for fleet operators in the future. It's easy to get depressed."

Having said that, Mike remains an optimist. "We are now a long way on from the proliferation of motor cruisers in the 1970s. In fact, in many places, especially on the Waveney, it's still like the 30s. The Waveney is a picture postcard idyll and has some of the best sailing waters in the Broads."

As we parted, he offered a definition: "You can always tell a Norfolk man - but you can't tell him much." Like all the best humour, it contains a truth beneath its patina of jocularity, for it captures the classic dilemma of the individual's battle to retain his identity in the face of the relentless onslaught of bureaucratic interference; and it might serve as a motto for the battle to save the Broads.

The marshes here are criss-crossed with a cat's cradle of high-tension power lines and pylons. These cables are a lethal obstacle to birds, many of them rare enough without having further perils put in their way. The wires have proved to be an especial hazard for marsh harriers, a potential disaster for the species because one third of the entire British breeding population is found in Norfolk. In an attempt to avert a crisis, the electricity board has opened a medical centre to treat harriers injured by these supercharged death-traps.

Haddiscoe has one of the most easily-visible churches on the marsh. This is rather apposite, for it contains a monument to Jan Piers, one of the army of Dutchmen who were ferried in from the Middle Ages onwards to drain the flood-plains.

Another monument to the men who reclaimed this landscape stands beside the river on the opposite bank: Herringfleet Mill. Built in 1820, it is Broadland's sole surviving timber smock mill that still has its canvas sails intact. These sails drove a 16ft scoop wheel and the mill was operated round the clock; a bed and hearth were fitted indoors. It would have be run by a marshman, whose other duties included reed-cutting, dyke-clearing, eel-catching and wildfowling; and the miller's lot was, in tempestuous weather, an alarming one: there are an abundance of stories of men trapped in mills that spun so wildly on their wind-controlled central pivots that sparks caused a conflagration and roasted the unhappy custodian.

Herringfleet Mill, like so many places along the Waveney, has an uninterrupted view of the marshes. The village from which it takes its name stands nearby and boasts one of the largest barns in Suffolk, a magnificent thatched edifice whose massive walls are a wondrous patchwork of brick and flint.

Somerleyton is renowned for its hall; but the village is also worth a look, a real curiosity of thatched cottages with maroon-painted half-timbering that even the normally loquacious Pevsner could describe only as "weird". The houses and church were built for the 19th century railway magnate Sir Morton Peto by John Thomas, who supplied the ornamental stonework for Charles Barry, architect of the Houses of Parliament. Thomas was also responsible for converting Somerleyton Hall for Peto from a Jacobean gem into a Victorian fantasy, much to the distaste of architectural purists. But even they would have to agree that the house contains much of fascination and beauty: a clock designed for the House of Commons but rejected because it was too expensive; carvings by the peerless Grinling Gibbons; and a sensational garden with, at its heart, what I consider to be the finest and most puzzling maze in Britain.

Peto was one of those Victorians who are regarded either as titans who put the Great into Britain or as grasping plutocrats who rose to power on the broken backs of their exploited workers. Certainly, Peto made a fortune, building railways as far afield as Russia and Argentina as well as at home. But it was a massively expensive and risky enterprise: the Yarmouth-Norwich line, built with George and Robert Stephenson of "Rocket" fame, cost £10,000 a mile, more than most people then could hope to earn in a lifetime. He also built Lowestoft harbour, the Reform Club and St James's Theatre in London and helped to finance Charles Barry. In the end, Peto overstretched himself and went spectacularly bust. He sold Somerleyton in 1861 to his friend and fellow nonconformist MP Francis Crossley, the leading carpet manufacturer in Halifax, West Yorkshire, who revolutionised his industry by installing Britain's first steam loom. Crossley and Peto had earlier collaborated with Prince Albert on the Great Exhibition.

The present Lord Somerleyton is the great-grandson of Francis and is acutely conscious of the ancestry that allowed him to be appointed Master of the Horse, one of three great Officers of State, and Lord-in-Waiting to the Queen. "We are immensely proud of our Halifax connections," he told me as we sat in his airy study overlooking the splendid

Lord Somerleyton

gardens. But this heritage brings huge responsibilities. "We have 5,000 acres here, 3,000 of which are farmed," he said. "It used to be bigger but we sold our land on the other side of the Waveney. There are now four tenant farms run by different families on the estate but when Father died in 1959 there were eight to ten more. It's terribly sad when old families go - it destroys the social fabric of the countryside."

He is in no doubt that landowners have a vital role to play in rural preservation. He said: "If it were not for big estates, the 'greens' would have a lot more to do. We produce beef, sugar beet, potatoes, wheat and barley but we also keep and cultivate our trees and hedgerows. We would never remove a hedge, so they are largely as they always were. The Government once paid people to pull them up and hedgerow deprivation has been awful in East Anglia. We kept ours because if you tore them all down it would be like living in a desert. There has to be a happy medium between profit and conservation. But I'm optimistic; it's not perfect but it's improving all the time."

Lord Somerleyton is not one of those landed gentry who believe their estates should be exclusive; indeed, he says the Country Landowners' Association has produced an initiative - called Access 2000 - to increase public rights of entrance in Britain. Although Somerleyton Hall is closed in the winter, miles of year-round footpaths traverse the estate and some 25,000 people come here in the visiting season. Another 100,000-odd visit Fritton. "We already have public access in an enormous way," he said, "and we don't feel in our case that we need to do any more. We are definitely doing our bit."

Visitors to the house are all struck by the two colossal stuffed polar bears that stand in the hallway, the trophies of an ancestor with a passion for arctic hunting. What they may not notice is the collection of china polar bears that adorn most of the surfaces around these monsters, a coterie put together by Lord Somerleyton in deference to his heritage. The house is a veritable treasure trove of furnishings and art that has been drawing people back to Somerleyton for decades. "But we are seeing big changes in the patterns of holidaymakers," Lord Somerleyton said. "Many now come to East Anglia for a long weekend instead of a fortnight. The snag is, of course, that the next stop after here is Holland."

The next stop on the Waveney, however, is not so distant. Oulton Broad is perhaps the busiest piece of water in the whole region, a situation exacerbated by the restoration of Mutford Lock which means that seagoing vessels can now join the crowds. It is hard to believe, looking at the chaos of powerboats, cruisers, yachts and dinghies on the broad today, that it was once a haven of peace. The Victorian writer and Bible-salesman George Borrow, who created the gipsy picaresques The Romany Rye and Lavengro, had an estate on the shore; the Edwardians held genteel "water frolics" here; and the lawyer and secret service agent Nicholas Everitt, who died in 1928, set up home here to write a series of books on wildfowling, including Broadland Sport. It is, however, still possible to catch glimpses of its former serenity: a

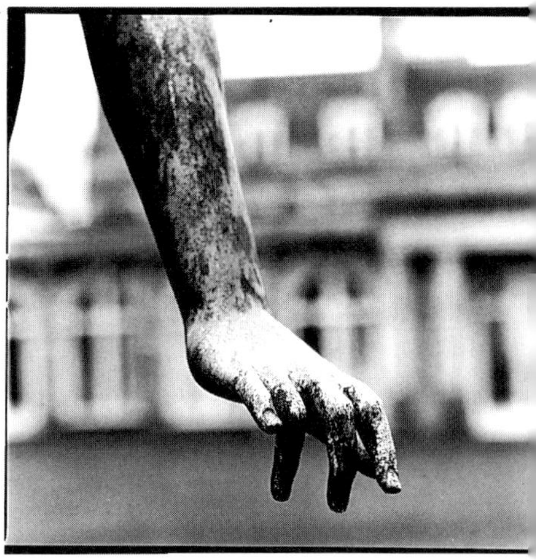

walk round the Suffolk Wildlife Trust's Carlton reserve is an exercise in tranquillity.

Better still, get back on the Waveney and pause at Burgh St Peter, a village with a lively marina and the most extraordinary church in the region. The main body of St Mary's is 13th century and is built in traditional stone with a thatched roof. But in 1793, a bizarre red brick tower, erected as a series of tapering steps, was tagged on. It was the brainchild of the local vicar, by name Boycott, who is thought to have been attempting (and, it has to be said, failing dismally) to recreate a tower seen on a Grand Tour of Europe. The Reverend Boycott was the second of five generations of his family to hold the living at Burgh St Peter; rather aptly, a descendant is still patron of the church. Incidentally, the verb "to boycott" owes its existence to another of the vicar's descendants, a land agent in Ireland in the 1880s who upset the locals so much with his sedulous acquisitiveness that he was universally cold-shouldered by the Irish.

The marina is part of the Waveney River Centre, which also features an indoor swimming pool, a campsite and a pub/restaurant, The Waveney Inn. It is owned by Tony Martin, a former accountant who spent 25 years abroad, mainly in the Near and Far East, before settling here in 1997.

"This is one of the less popular parts of the Broads," he said, "although I have no idea why because it is one of the prettiest and has the best sailing. Wroxham and Horning feel like the M25 at the height of the season but this is really quite isolated. There are about one and half times more boats on the northern rivers than on the Waveney because they were developed earlier and because there are more broads and villages - Oulton and Beccles are the only significant waterside settlements here. But it means we have few troublemakers, even though the fleshpots of Oulton are only a short distance away."

Tony started sailing on the Broads as a ten-year-old on family holidays. "I was overseas for many years," he said, "but 17 years ago we bought a cottage at Stokesby which we still have - it's a handy bolthole. My wife always wanted to run a restaurant and I fancied playing around with boats so we came here. We feel very comfortable in Norfolk."

The Waveney Inn has stood here for at least 150 years and the river centre has been in existence for about 30 years. In its early days the restaurant was a separate building used as a family room as well as a venue for bingo and weekend discos. Nowadays, the marina offers 110 permanent moorings, berths for 50 or 60 visiting boats, static caravans and a camping and caravan park on a 16-acre site that has its own discreet sewage works. In theory, the centre can accommodate up to 1,000 people.

"We are open all year," Tony said, "but the season proper starts around Easter. We employ about 25 staff at the peak, mainly in the restaurant, but a lot depends on the weather. If it is kind, we still have people in November and more and more people venture out in winter because motorboats in particular are becoming increasingly sophisticated."

Tourist numbers are good at present but they would tumble if rumours that the New Cut is earmarked for closure prove true. "It could have a devastating effect because any boat that can't get under St Olave's bridge won't get here. Now that Mutford Lock has been restored, we get quite a few coastal boats, some from as far away as Holland and Germany, but unless they can cross Oulton Broad (maximum depth 6ft) they can't reach us either. We have a 44ft motorboat moored here which can cross the broad but a 44ft yacht draws a minimum of six to seven feet and wouldn't manage it."

Meanwhile, maintaining the river centre is a year-round task. In fact, says Tony, running the site is not unlike painting the Forth Bridge: the work never stops. "We have more than enough business to keep us fully occupied," he said. "There is always something to do - piling, road-mending, maintenance."

Piling is a subject of some friction. He said: "The Broads Authority is mad keen on wood piling, although I think that's environmentally suspect. We are mad keen on steel. It costs a bit more but it lasts much longer."

Tony's local problem reflects one that is common throughout the region. The Broads Authority is anxious to have natural-looking banks and has been experimenting with such diverse forms of protection as netting and copra, none of which has the same life expectancy as steel. But they are cheaper, in the short term at any rate, and that counts for a lot when bank erosion is so widespread. For example, 1996 figures revealed that some 150 miles of banking would need to be repaired over the following decade at an estimated cost of £63million. Piling prices at that time were between £800 and £1,300 a metre for steel and between £200 and £500 for alder wood. Not only does the latter look prettier, it also satisfies the demands of the accountants - and thus makes it the perfect solution for any self-respecting bureaucrat.

My own preference is for copra or netting because both allow reeds to regain a foothold in the shallows and thus provide the most efficient and aesthetic form of protection. This is not always possible on rivers but I hope it will eventually replace all the ugly old piling that has been used in stop-gap repairs on some of the quieter stretches of Broadland's waterways.

eleven

The river now swings west, passing landlocked Barnby Broad - the only other broad on the Waveney - before reaching Beccles, a Norman seaport that is today eight miles from the coast. A new bridge carries the main road over the river but the old, low bridge still stands. In former times, wherrymen bypassed it in times of flood by sailing across the inundated water meadows that surround the town. Beccles is full of Georgian houses and narrow streets and is renowned for its parish church of St

Michael's with its separate 97ft tower. Nearby is a plaque to Professor Dame Dorothy Hodgkin, a crystallographer who became one of the most celebrated scientists of the century, if not of all time. She was born in the town in 1910 and during the next 84 years helped to save millions of lives by discovering the molecular structure of penicillin, insulin and the anti-anaemia vitamin B12. Her work won her the Nobel Prize for Chemistry in 1964 and the Order of Merit. She was the only woman apart from Florence Nightingale to have been awarded the OM at the time.

St Michael's is one of the biggest churches in Broadland - and thus needs more upkeep than most. The Rev Andrew Thomas, the rector, has the task of balancing the needs of the past with those of the present and future. "This church is a bit of a barn-like place," he said, "and it is very expensive to look after. The whole thing would cost about £350,000 if we did everything that needs to be done. As it is, we must raise about £200,000." St Michael's is a Grade One listed building, which entitles it to a grant of 40 per cent of the costs from English Heritage. "But," Andrew pointed out, "the Government take 17 per cent of that grant straight back in VAT. It's a nonsense."

The church is 14th century but contains much that is newer, such as a 20th century screen. "It's a bit like being a museum curator running this place," Andrew said. And this is the dilemma: Retaining the old while trying to keep the church relevant. "Take the screen," he said. "It's fine if you like that sort of thing; but I would prefer it if the altar was not cut off from the body of the church. We

The Rev Andrew Thomas

have to attract more young people. A report said the Church was haemorrhaging 1,000 youngsters a week - and that trend has to be reversed. Updated language has helped and we have started a more modern Sunday service. But many of the congregation are very traditional, so the message is 'Be gentle.' We can't expect dramatic changes, just quiet progress through word-of-mouth networking."

Andrew began his clerical career as a curate in Cromer, later progressing to be a vicar near King's Lynn and finally spending 12 years in the London suburbs at Cheam, immortalised as the fictional home of Tony Hancock. "We had lots of young, highly mobile people in Cheam," he recalled, "and we were very successful. We raised congregation numbers and we raised £1.2million to build a new church. Beccles is very different."

St Michael's is enjoying more success than many other Broadland parishes, however. Dozens have been combined as congregation numbers fall until, in some cases, one priest is looking after half a dozen churches. Andrew has a team vicar who takes care of St Luke's, a more modern church on a former council estate in the town, and was awaiting the arrival of a curate, the first in Beccles for more than three decades. Congregation numbers remain solid. "We get more than 100 at morning service on Sunday, with another 30 or so in the evening and at 8am Holy Communion. There are a few youngsters but mostly they are older people, which I suppose mirrors the age range in Beccles. When I was at Cromer, the numbers used to swell by two or three hundred in the summer but here it is up by dozens rather than hundreds. The trouble is, we are a long way from anywhere else in the Broads by water."

What is trouble for the church is, ironically, good news for everyone else, for it means that this part of Broadland is not overwhelmed by crowds. Big boats can press on for a short time until the head of navigation at Shipmeadow Lock in Geldeston, which has been disused since 1934. But those of us in canoes can - and should - continue to Ditchingham and Bungay, even though the river is now beyond the bounds of the national park.

Ditchingham was once home to Ancient British tribes who built long-barrow graves, one of which has been dated at 3,500BC. It was also home to Sir Henry Rider Haggard, whose novel King Solomon's Mines entranced generations of schoolboys. Despite his fame as a writer, Haggard was foremost a farmer; he earned his knighthood for his work with a Royal Commission on forestry and agriculture. He was also an ardent and highly effective campaigner against marathon church sermons. Every Sunday, as the preacher rose to the pulpit, he placed a pile of half-crowns on his pew and removed one coin every 15 minutes. Whatever remained when the sermon finished was placed in the collection box. Ditchingham preachers soon learned the art of succinctness.

Bungay, whose Saxon spirit lives on in the title of its mayor, Town Reeve, has many splendid houses, a 1689 Butter Cross built above a dungeon and a fine twin-towered Norman castle that was given to the town in 1987 by the Duke of Norfolk. Bungay's oldest building is Holy Trinity church, which was the scene in 1577 of a demonic visit: a huge dog with saucer-like eyes and jangling chains burst into the nave during an apocalyptic thunderstorm and killed two burghers at prayer. The hound is variously called Black Shuck, Old Scarp and Owd Rugason.

My journey ended, appropriately enough, at Earsham, where the Otter Trust has been based since 1975. Philip and Jeanne Wayre breed these rare mammals and release them into the wild at secret locations. When the couple began, the otter population in Norfolk was reduced to single figures; at the time of writing, it is more than a hundred.

The otter seems to me as good a metaphor as any for the beauty and the hope I found throughout my travels in Broadland. Whether the region will become healthy enough to allow otters to flourish remains to be seen, for only the most jejune commentator would suggest that conservation will win its contest for supremacy against economic interests simply because it must. But otter tracks have been seen at Sir John Blofeld's estate on the Bure and there have been sightings on and around the Ted Ellis Trust on the Yare, two of the busiest spots in the entire Broadland river system. There has also been marked progress in the recovery of such rarities as kites, ospreys, marsh harriers and bearded tits, water soldiers, orchids and marsh peas, swallowtail butterflies, the Norfolk aeshna and galeruca interrupta beetles, not to mention molluscs and other lesser-known life-forms. These are just a few examples - and they offer considerable grounds for optimism.

At the same time, however, the decline of the bittern seems terminal, eels are vanishing, river banks continue to be washed away as boat numbers soar; and over all this, the menace of a rise in sea levels caused by spiralling - and apparently ignored - global warming hangs like an environmental sword of Damocles.

Of course, the forces of nature will in some future epoch obliterate Broadland, however hard we fight. But in the centuries before that need happen, the evanescent wetland requires more than anything the dedicated toil of its devotees backed up by a bureaucratically-driven commercial sea-change that inspires - and finances - a switch from short-term monetary considerations to long-term vision in order to bridge the gulf that currently separates the worlds of economics and ecology.

Cynics will argue that such sentiments are simplistic and idealistic. Possibly... but that does not mean they are unworkable. And anyway, it seems to me that a bit of simplicity mixed with a generous dose of idealism is the best possible antidote to the administrative complexities that today prevent so many people seeing the wood for the trees - or the wonder for the amenity. The truth is that the gulf must be bridged because only then may we begin to believe that the Broads have turned not just a corner, but the corner. And what better moment to make that turn than now, at the start of a new millennium?

The publishers would like to thank all those who were interviewed for the book and who made Still Waters possible by giving so generously of their time and knowledge. Maas would also like to thank Eve Hedley, Mrs Thompson at Neatishead, Lucy Williams at the Broads Authority, Nick Hedley for his invaluable technical assistance, John Nickalls and Clive Hedley.